GEN X PITTSBURGH

THE BEEHIVE
AND THE '90s SCENE

DAVID RULLO

THE
History
PRESS

Published by The History Press
Charleston, SC
www.historypress.com

Copyright © 2023 by David Rullo
All rights reserved

Opposite: Still taken from a video recorded by Terence Lee.

First published 2023

Manufactured in the United States

ISBN 9781467153744

Library of Congress Control Number: 2023940703

To my wife, Kim, and son, Jack.
Kim, you have always allowed me to follow my dreams, of which you are the greatest. Thank you for giving me the space needed to write this book.
Jack, I hope you, too, will find a place as wonderful as the Beehive to misspend some of your youth.

And of course, to Ant, Greg, Rob and Z—the original crew, with whom I discovered the Beehive and spent far too many hours.

A big city is not like a small town. In a small town, a person goes out of his house and immediately finds his friend; in a big city days and weeks and months may go by until they see one another, and so they set up a special place in the coffeehouse where they drop in at appointed times.

—*Shmuel Yosef,* Only Yesterday

CONTENTS

ACKNOWLEDGEMENTS

This is a book of memories. In the course of writing it, I interviewed over seventy people, some multiple times. I have done over one hundred interviews. As a result, not every interview I conducted was used. Some had to be left out for space, and others weren't included because they covered the same ground.

In many ways, the story of the Beehive is one of time and place. It could only have happened when it did and where it did. It was a pioneer in the changing South Side neighborhood. I tried to capture those changes through the stories of those with whom I spoke. Whenever possible, I let people tell their own stories and highlight the evolution of the South Side from a community existing in the shadows of a steel mill—both real and imagined—to an arts community that organically grew over time. As a result, this book is part investigative journalism, part oral history and part historical document.

If any of the details are incorrect, these errors can be attributed to the writer and my misunderstanding of the details told to me.

And while I have worked to string together a narrative of memories, they are, of course, mere vignettes of a time. It is impossible to capture all the memories and the value of the Beehive in people's lives in a book this size.

Every interview I did was valuable, but there were a few people who went above and beyond in their willingness to share and help. Credit first has to go to the Beehive's owners, Scott Kramer and Steve Zumoff. They were open, giving and willing to share both their memories and homes with a writer they only met when I approached the pair about writing the book. Valerie Gatchell-Christofel was a treasure trove of information, providing names, contact information, connections and memories. Her excitement for this book was only overshadowed by my own. Nikole Boyda McGuinness was generous to a fault with both her time and photographs. Bob Ziller and Andrew Laswell both sat for multiple interviews, making connections where possible and working to untangle the multiple threads of community at the Beehive. Terence Lee graciously shared with me the interviews he recorded during the final week of the Beehive's operation, and the Heinz History Center of Pittsburgh provided the spellings of the names of everyone whom I interviewed. Lastly, Toby Tabachnick, my editor at the *Pittsburgh Jewish Chronicle*, was the first to read my manuscript and offer suggestions and edits.

Thanks to everyone with whom I spoke. This book is only possible because of your generosity.

A sketch and poem made at the Oakland Beehive. *From Nikole Boyda McGuinness, private collection.*

INTRODUCTION

T he Beehive changed my life."
      I heard that refrain over and over while writing this book. Artists, photographers, mothers, musicians, circus performers and neighborhood denizens all said the same thing.

I believed them because the Beehive changed my life.

In 1990, I was a freshman at Point Park College, located on the Boulevard of the Allies in downtown Pittsburgh. The city hadn't yet recovered from the collapse of the steel industry, and the blocks around the school were vacant. A Rax Roast Beef, McDonalds and Subway were all that was available if one wanted a quick meal. There were few art galleries and only a Walden Book Store several blocks away. There was no nightlife or cultural district of which to speak. Even Starbucks was several years away from reaching the city.

Point Park College, not yet a university, was an extremely liberal place of higher learning, bordering on an art school. It was known for its journalism, dance and acting majors and not much more. Its three buildings housed most of its students, as well as artists in training from the nearby Art Institute of Pittsburgh and Pittsburgh Filmmakers. I was studying to be a writer; my friends were musicians and filmmakers. I dated an artist. We hung out with photographers, ballet dancers, future directors and radio personalities in wait. Outside of the school, however, there was little to do during our off-hours. It would be charitable to call the underground art and literature scene downtown and in the nearby South Side and North Side neighborhoods burgeoning.

That was soon to change.

In 1991, the '90s hadn't yet started. The calendar might have alleged it to be the ninth decade of the twentieth century, but that was purely coincidental.

When the Beehive opened its doors, six months after I started my freshman year, Pittsburgh was still best known for its failing steel mills, polluted air, once dominant football team and colloquial accent. Generation X and the youth transformation that came with it wasn't yet part of the cultural zeitgeist. And yet, a funny thing happened on the way to the stadium; the coffeehouse found a loyal and large customer base with virtually no advertising or promotion. Kids with green hair, tattoos, ripped jeans and pierced noses starting showing up in a neighborhood not yet known as ground zero in the city's art scene.

The Beehive became, if you'll excuse the pun, a hive of social activity before the advent of social media. Artists began calling the café home, musicians spent time there between gigs and college students started and ended their nights at the coffeehouse. An ethos formed both inside and outside the walls of the espresso bar.

To those who weren't part of the scene, the clientele was something new for Pittsburgh's South Side neighborhood. They didn't fit in with the shot-and-beer mentality built around the neighborhood. They took parking spaces, were loud and ignorant, didn't wear Steelers or Pirates caps and certainly didn't look like the good kids the neighborhood had raised who attended city or Catholic schools.

That was only one side of the story though.

For those in the know and for that first generation of Beehives customers, the coffeehouse was a place where they could find others like themselves. Outside, they might have been considered freaks and losers, but inside, they found fraternity and sorority. They could talk about music and art. They didn't seem pretentious or weird. They found their tribe.

A simmering tension existed between the neighborhood and the caffeine-based establishment until those living near the café began to slowly, begrudgingly accept that their once cloistered neighborhood was becoming the artsy hangout for a group of Pittsburghers. Their once deserted storefronts would begin to be populated by businesses with a similar vibe—Slacker, Groovy, the Culture Shop, the Lava Lounge—even formerly safe environs like Dee's Café would shake off the last vestiges of their industrial past and welcome a new generation.

I wasn't aware of the social impact of the Beehive when I found it. I simply knew I discovered a place where I fit in.

I had grown up mostly in Western Pennsylvania suburbs, with a brief New England stopover. My parents and the parents of my friends were either the first generation not working in a mine, steel mill or industrial plant or had recently become unemployed from a mine, steel mill or industrial plant and were still figuring out what that meant.

I wasn't supposed to aspire to be a writer. I certainly wasn't supposed to have my hair fashioned in a skater's cut, wear a three-quarter-length leather coat that I picked up in a thrift shop, spend my time visiting bookstores and record stores trying to find out-of-print editions of Jack Kerouac novels or Charlie Parker imports and seeking out others who existed on the margins of society. It was expected that I would keep my head down, get a degree in something sensible, like business, and come back to the suburbs to start a career in insurance. If I couldn't do that, I was expected to end up a janitor in one of the local hospitals.

And I may have ended up back living in one of the Monongahela Valley towns until white flight pushed me farther east to a more rural suburb like North Huntington or Greensburg.

The Beehive changed that.

I had already found other kids like me at Point Park, but I thought that might have been a fluke. But once we walked into the South Side coffeehouse on a Friday night, I knew I wasn't alone.

The artwork was vaguely West Coast, and the customers had dreadlocks or dyed hair. They wore clothes like mine. They seemed slightly older, more urbane. It took about thirty seconds for me to realize I would be spending time at this place and the neighborhood where it was situated.

What I didn't know was that the coffeehouse would become Pittsburgh's center for the grunge and Gen X culture soon to become part of the American psyche. These people, in their ripped jeans, Doc Martens and cardigan sweaters were similar to those in the scenes developing in most large cities.

This cultural phenomenon happened without the internet, cellphones, Facebook, Twitter, Instagram or TikTok. It was almost completely free of cross-pollination from other cities, but it was completely consistent with what was occurring in Seattle, Portland, Austin, New York and most other large metropolitan areas.

It would sweep my generation into its vortex.

Like it did for so many others, the Beehive changed my life.

It changed the lives of many of the people interviewed for this book. It also changed Pittsburgh. It was partly responsible for establishing the South

The Beehive's sign. *Scott Kramer and Steve Zumoff, private collection.*

Side neighborhood as an artistic haven. Bands on local labels, like Blue Duck Records, not only frequented the coffeehouse, but they also performed at Club Café and the Lava Lounge, Nick's Fat City and Graffiti. Shops like Slacker and Groovy appealed to those who were looking for underground wear and retro fashion. Dee's Café provided cheap alcohol. Across a bridge and down the road, another Beehive and Slacker, located in the college neighborhood of Oakland, offered movies, poetry readings and coffee. Tela Ropa sold velvet Day-Glo posters and bongs. The Avalon offered upscale but still inexpensive versions of the clothes found in thrift shops and Salvation Army stores, and the Upstage spun gothic and industrial dance music.

It would take another decade for Pittsburgh to become known as a travel destination for foodies or to start redeveloping its downtown area into a cultural nightspot with attractive loft living. Those changes can be traced directly to a coffeehouse in a neighborhood that was expected to offer nothing more to its out-of-work steel workers than a local shot-and-beer hole in the wall where they could watch the Steelers, Pirates or Penguins sweat it out. The Beehive changed the energy of a city. It changed its DNA. It created a scene.

1

PRE-HIVE

Standing on the corner of Fourteenth and East Carson Streets, the Beehive Coffeehouse and Dessertery was hard to miss.

Painted in vibrant primary colors with a yellow logo that featured an image of a woman sporting the dated hairdo that shares the name of the café, the Beehive seemed better suited for San Francisco or Greenwich Village than Pittsburgh's South Side.

Given its looks and wares—espresso and cappuccino drinks priced at a premium in a neighborhood better known for its shots and beers—the Beehive seemed destined to fail before it ever launched.

Lisa Young, a longtime friend of co-owner Scott Kramer, expressed doubts when she learned of the new café from her friend. "I told him, how are you ever going to make money with a coffee shop, but he said, 'No, it's a real thing. We went across the country and to other cities, and there's coffee shops in them.' I said, 'OK, good luck with that.'"

Those fears were alleviated in February 1991, when the Beehive opened its doors. A large and soon-to-be-loyal clientele filled the shop in its first few hours of operation.

"I remember there was a line around the block," Kramer recalled.

Scott had conceptualized the coffeehouse with his business partner, Steve Zumoff. The pair decided to gamble on coffee and rich desserts in a city that was the home of ex–steel workers and third-generation immigrant families from Eastern Europe and Italy. And while the idea and location might not sound so outlandish today, in the early '90s, Pittsburgh had none of the

The Beehive's logo before it was hung on the building's façade. *Photograph provided by Scott Kramer and Steve Zumoff.*

hipster or foodie trappings that would soon see it named one of the country's most livable cities.

The original business plan articulated modest goals for the new café. "Said business is intended to be a coffee shop with unique features that would differentiate it from other businesses located in the area," Kramer and Zumoff wrote. The coffeehouse was "intended to create a 'Bohemian' atmosphere. Persons regarded as bohemians are traditionally those with artistic and literary interests who disregard conventional standards of behavior."

Steve and Scott's vision might have seemed a stretch given the Reagan-esque feel that still dominated much of the country, but there were signs that things were beginning to change.

In 1990, the *New York Times* ran a story by Margot Slade, titled "Campus Cafes Attract 'Neo-Beatniks.'" In it, she wrote that "new and newly popular coffeehouses are serving up poetry and progressive music in rooms heavy with smoke and intellectual pretension."

The Beehive's early clientele were Pittsburgh's "neo-beatniks": artists and art students, those studying at nearby colleges and universities, musicians, writers, filmmakers, out-of-work ne'er-do-wells and those still trying to find their way.

While society may have been struggling with labels for this new generation at the time—*slackers*, *bohos* and other names were bandied about—there was no denying the initial stirrings of Generation X in the city. This group would eventually help transform Pittsburgh from its industrial past to a future that included an economy based on technology, healthcare, universities and hip restaurants, an expanding art scene, vibrant downtown living and converted brown spaces.

Two regions were instrumental in reimaging Pittsburgh: Oakland and the South Side. Home to the University of Pittsburgh, Carnegie Mellon University and Carlow College (now Carlow University), plus several hospitals, Oakland was an incubator for the city and its young, hip students. The South Side, on the other hand, offered cheap rent, underground art galleries and studios and access to downtown, and it was near Point Park College (now Point Park University) and the Art Institute of Pittsburgh. Both offered frequent buses and walkable communities.

Scott and Steve first imagined the Beehive at a location on Atwood Street in Oakland. It made sense—the two had attended college at the University

The espresso bar's pricing sign. *Scott Kramer and Steve Zumoff, private collection.*

Various photographs of Scott and Steve. The two seemed older to their employees but were usually only five to seven years older than them. *Photographs by Nikole Boyda McGuinness.*

of Pittsburgh, lived nearby in the city's East End and were enthused by the university district that seemed ready-made for a coffee revolution.

When the location fell through, the pair shifted their focus to the other side of the Monongahela River—East Carson Street in the city's South Side neighborhood. In the process, they and the organic growth around their coffee shop helped the struggling community develop something it needed for more than a decade—an identity.

The Beehive and the businesses that opened around it—Slacker, Groovy, Dee's Café and more—helped it identify itself as both a home to the nascent '90s art scene and an entertainment destination. It was able to do this at a time when much of the city was fighting to claw its way back from the collapse of the steel industry.

To fight this postindustrial morass, Pittsburgh mayor Richard Caliguiri developed a plan he called "Renaissance II," meant to address the deindustrialization with bold initiatives.

Caligiuri's blueprint reimagined the city's physical landscape, adding landmarks like the all-glass PPG Place and One Oxford Center. By the time of his death in 1988, the success that was beginning to be felt downtown hadn't yet made it to neighborhoods like Lawrenceville or Bloomfield, and it would never touch some of the areas surrounding Pittsburgh. Five decades after most of the steel mills closed, the rails and barges filled with coal ceased deliveries and the last miner clocked out, cities like McKeesport, Duquesne and Braddock are still waiting for their redevelopment opportunities.

East Carson Street, the main thoroughfare through the South Side, would become home to art studios and galleries, coffeehouses, vintage clothing boutiques catering to an alternative audience, concert venues, high-end condominiums, restaurants, dive bars, sports bars, Irish bars, hookah bars and virtually any other type of bar that could be imagined. Before any of those other businesses existed, however, there was the Beehive, which found fortune on its opening day.

The coffeehouse proved to be so successful that on most weeknights and through the weekends, if you didn't arrive early enough, you didn't get a seat.

Customers often stood three deep because the tables were filled. Those who arrived early in the day or never left occupied the mismatched tables and chairs along the right wall of the café. A huddled mass stood next to the filled seats, balancing mugs of coffee and cappuccinos, waiting to pounce on a table if anyone seated left. A third line stood in front of the counter, ordering drinks and desserts or chatting with baristas.

At the front of the coffeehouse, a round table was situated in a window space. It became premium seating that was typically filled by regulars or special guests like the Red Hot Chili Peppers.

A hive begins to form. *Photograph provided by Scott Kramer and Scott Zumoff.*

Customers waiting in line at South Side Beehive. *Photograph by Karen Lillis.*

A Beehive bathroom. *Photograph by David Grim.*

Pinball at the South Hills location. *Photograph provided by Scott Kramer and Steve Zumoff.*

In the rear of the café, people played pinball. Remarkably, the Beehive had done the near impossible and made playing the analog game popular again. In the years to come, Steve would play an integral role in revitalizing pinball culture throughout the region.

Others were content to stand in the open space, leaving little to no room between them for anyone who needed to visit the highly graffitied bathrooms.

The coffeehouse became a viable third space for many Pittsburgh Gen Xers, who used it as a place to plan artistic collaborations, play pinball, chess or *Magic: The Gathering*. It was also a place where customers could discuss theater, read a book from one of the shelves located in the space, meet before a party or simply get together in the pre-internet days to share a sense of community.

Before there was a Starbucks on every corner, before a sitcom featuring six friends that hung out at a local coffeehouse ever aired, before alternative culture became pop culture and before Pittsburgh began landing on the top of "Best of Cities to Live" lists, the Beehive brought coffee culture, and with it a healthy dose of art and alternative lifestyles, to the Steel City.

SCOTT AND STEVE DECIDED to create a coffeehouse that catered to an artsy clientele while they traveled across the country to attend a Jerry Garcia concert. The two had met as students at the University of Pittsburgh—Scott was a business major, and Steve studied psychology and worked at Zelda's, a destination bar for many Pitt students, where Scott often stopped for a drink. It was at another Oakland bar, Thirsty's, during the watering hole's regular Grateful Dead night that the two first discussed the idea of opening a coffeehouse together.

Scott's objective was clear from an early age: to be an entrepreneur and find some way to combine that goal with art. He started young, selling flavored ice cubes at Taylor Allderdice High School's baseball field before moving on to cutting grass in the city's East End, where he grew up. He kept his landscaping business while in college before adding the unusual title of tie-dye T-shirt creator and distributor to his resumé.

Rather than sell the T-shirts he was making door to door or in stores, Scott found a distributor in New York that sold the shirts to other companies. The shirts were so well received that several rock bands bought them to use—after printing their logos on them—as tour shirts. After receiving word that the dye he used in his shirts was carcinogenic, Scott shut down the space he had stacked with washers, laid off his few employees and began thinking about his next business venture.

It was a New England sales representative Scott had hired to sell his shirts who first mentioned he had noticed coffeehouses opening up in a few cities throughout the United States. "He told me that coffee was going to be big and asked me to make tie-dyed T-shirts that they could sell in coffee shops." Kramer remembered. "It was an idea I bounced off of Steve, and then, traveling across the country to see the Dead, we started checking out coffeehouses."

In the 2,400-plus miles between Pittsburgh and Los Angeles, the pair decided a coffeehouse was at least something they should consider. In Chicago, they took particular note of one new chain that hadn't yet reached the East Coast.

BY THE LATE '80s, coffee was beginning to come into its own in America. Manufacturers were starting to experiment with various flavors, enticing those who weren't fans of the acrid brew straight, and some cafés were selling a new addition to their line of caffeinated drinks: iced coffees. Of course, once a Washington store decided to create a chain, coffee, it seemed, found its footing.

Opened in Seattle in 1971, Starbucks had expanded to the Windy City by the next decade. The coffeehouse was proof that patrons desired cafés where they could buy Americanized versions of European espresso drinks and desserts and hang out for hours at a time. The coffeehouses revitalized the idea of '60s cafés like those found in Greenwich Village, where folk troubadours performed and radicals argued their beliefs. Starbucks found a way to make the coffeehouse safe for the suburbs. And while Scott and Steve weren't yet sure they would be opening a coffeehouse—they weren't even coffee drinkers—they did take note of the growing scene and menu at Starbucks.

Steve told Scott about Shapiro's Coffee, a shop in Lemoyne, Pennsylvania, near Harrisburg, where he had grown up, that had been in business for more than a decade. Kramer remembered the café as something between the more traditional diner and college coffeehouse.

In 1990, the two took one last decisive trip, traveling to Toronto, Canada. It was there, after visiting Just Desserts, an establishment Steve recalled from a trip north in the '80s, that served multiple types of tea, that they settled on opening a coffeehouse.

The voyage north provided more than simply inspiration, Steve recalled. The city had a bar on Queen's Street with an unusual name that caught both Steve's and Scott's eye—the Beehive. The saloon was open for only approximately two months and was best remembered for its connection to the Pittsburgh coffeehouse. "I think there was a display outside made from a bunch of Bic lighters," Steve remembered. "It was really colorful."

The name, Scott and Steve would find out shortly after opening, had wings with more than their coffeehouse. A Pittsburgh strip club had opened with the same name before going out of business. "We used to get calls for it from time to time. That was interesting." Scott recalled, "We would sometimes get people asking if certain girls were working. We would tell the caller the girl had the night off."

Those early trips proved useful for the partners, who found inspiration for other aspects of their future coffeehouse.

Kramer remembered that in Toronto, the buildings were colorful. In Harrisburg, patrons poured coffee from French presses. In Chicago, they found a pamphlet in Starbucks that explained how to make the perfect cappuccino. They also began learning about roasting beans and initiated the task of deciding which coffee brand they liked best.

After their Oakland location fell through, Scott thought back to the South Side, an area he had previously visited when considering a few possible

BEEHIVE COFFEE FACTS

1) SOME COFFEE PLANTS REACH A HEIGHT OF TWENTY FEET OR MORE.

2) COFFEE WAS FIRST DISCOVERED BY A YOUNG ETHIOPIAN GOAT HERDER WHO NOTICED HIS HERD BOUNDING ABOUT THE HILLSIDE IN A STRANGE MANNER AFTER THEY HAD EATEN CHERRIES FROM THE THEN UNFAMILIAR SHRUB.

3) THE FIRST COFFEEHOUSES, CALLED "KAHUCH KANES" BY THE TURKS, WERE OPENED IN MECCA. STUDENTS, TRAVELLERS, MUSICIANS AND STORYTELLERS GATHERED TO SING, PLAY GAMES, DANCE, TALK AND, OF COURSE, DRINK COFFEE.

4) COFFEE WAS ONCE CONSIDERED A NESCESITY FOR LIFE. AT TURKISH WEDDING CEREMONIES, MEN HAD TO PROMISE TO PROVIDE THE DRINK FOR THEIR WIVES. FAILURE TO DO SO COULD BE GROUNDS FOR DIVORCE.

5) IN SEVENTEENTH CENTURY CONSTANTINOPLE, COFFEEHOUSES AND COFFEE CONSUMPTION WAS ILLEGAL. FIRST TIME OFFENDERS WERE BEATEN, WHILE SECOND TIME VIOLATORS WERE SEWN INTO LEATHER BAGS AND TOSSED IN THE OCEAN. SERIOUSLY.

6) COFFEE IN EUROPE WAS ORIGINALLY THOUGHT TO BE THE DRINK OF *SATAN*. ONE DAY, THE POPE TRIED A CUP. HIS REPLY? " WE SHALL FOOL SATAN BY BAPTIZING IT AND CREATING A TRULY CHRISTIAN BEVERAGE." SO HE DID.

7) IT HAS BEEN SUGGESTED BY SOME FRENCH PHYSICIANS THAT GARGLING WITH COFFEE CAN IMPROVE THE VOICE.

8) THE SPEECH THAT PRECIPITATED THE FALL OF THE BASTILLE IN PARIS TOOK PLACE IN A COFFEEHOUSE.

9) THERE ARE TWO MAJOR SPECIES OF COFFEE: ROBUSTO AND ARABICA, WITH ARABICA BEING THE SUPERIOR. ARABICA BEANS HAVE A MUCH BETTER FLAVOR BUT ROBUSTO BEANS, ON AVERAGE, PACK ALMOST TWICE THE CAFFEINE.

10) THE BOSTON TEA PARTY WAS PLANNED BY THE LIKES OF JOHN ADAMS AND PAUL REVERE IN A BOSTON COFFEEHOUSE CALLED THE GREEN DRAGON.

11) TEA LEAVES CONTAIN TWICE AS MUCH CAFFEINE AS DO COFFEEBEANS. AT THE SAME TIME, HOWEVER, IT TAKES ALMOST FOUR TIMES AS MUCH COFFEE, BY DRY WEIGHT, TO MAKE A PALATABLE CUP.

Coffee facts curated for Beehive employees. *Scott Kramer and Steve Zumoff, private collection.*

real estate investments. While that particular venture never materialized, he thought it might provide a home for the Beehive. "We came across the location," he said, "called the landlord, who said it was available. He said, 'I'll do the electric, and I'll do the heating and air conditioning, and I'll charge you guys like $1,100 or $1,200 dollars a month.' We took it."

The Beehive, preconstruction. *Photograph provided by Scott Kramer and Scott Zumoff.*

Landos drugstore. *Scott Kramer and Steve Zumoff, private collection.*

The neighborhood, Steve said, wasn't a last resort, but it was fairly close to a final destination. "Maybe it's because we were young and not yet a business, but no one wanted to rent us property. The South Side was still pretty run down," he said. "It hadn't yet become what it is today."

The storefront they finally rented had been Lando's Pharmacy in its previous incarnation, and it wasn't in great shape when the two agreed to lease it. Inside, along with pounds of asbestos that needed to be removed, were remnants of the building's former life, including shelves and counters, which found use as part of the coffeehouse.

Scott and Steve, as well as their new landlord, who worked as a contractor, rehabbed the building and began creating the design of the iconic café.

The total amount invested was close to $28,000, Scott said. To help recoup the money they put in, they secured a bank loan of $10,000. That money paid for the rent of the building; the equipment, coffee and supplies needed to open; the furniture; and even the plumbing and carpentry.

Like the building, the Beehive's original espresso machine had seen better days, or as Scott remembered, "It was a piece of garbage. We paid $2,500 for it. It was the most expensive thing we bought and in three or six months we had to buy a new one."

TIM KAULEN IS THE founder and executive director of Industrial Arts Workshop, a not-for-profit that works to inspire artistic literacy by offering enrichment opportunities that advance the understanding and process of sculpture-making artists and their works. In the early 1990s, however, he was a recent graduate of the Art Institute of Pittsburgh and a street artist creating works inspired by and part of the city's post-industrial landscape. He was also an important link between the South Side that existed before the Beehive and what it involved into after the coffeehouse had opened. "There was community there," Tim said of the neighborhood pre-Beehive. "It had all the amenities there which allowed it to be a cohesive community with a real culture and real tradition and real character." He said that while the South Side was affected by the collapse of the steel industry, it never fell into the complete disrepair of other neighboring communities.

It was that foundation of essential businesses, Tim ventured, that saved the area from total collapse. "There were no chain stores; everything was mom and pop–run businesses—a couple of bakeries, a poultry shop, a couple of used bookstores, there were a couple of art galleries," he said. That didn't save it from experiencing some of the blight felt by areas like

Hazelwood, especially after J&L Steel Works closed its mill on the banks of the Monongahela River in 1987.

In some ways, he said, the South Side of the late '80s and early '90s was trapped in another time. As an example, he cited the realty company from which he rented his apartment. The front office was staffed by two men with tight crew cuts who wore short-sleeve button shirts and ties. "It was literally like walking into the 1950s," Tim said. "When I wrote a check, they corrected me on exactly how to print the name and numbers. They schooled me every step of the way."

Tim found the South Side, which would soon be home to the Beehive, a welcome place for both the existing community and the boarded-up buildings and empty lots that would soon play an important role in the art he would create.

A forgotten relic—a pay phone. The mostly extinct devices were popular at the Beehive. *Photograph by Nikole Boyda McGuinness.*

IT WAS IN THIS neighborhood that the Beehive was born. Scott would earn the respect of many of the coffeehouse's neighbors by going door to door, introducing himself and telling them of the plans he and Steve had for the storefront. At the top of his list at the moment, however, was the daunting task of redesigning the interior of the building, creating a logo and letter mark for the new business and getting art on the walls. For that, they would turn to a nearby resource: the artists and students already living on the South Side.

2

ARTISTS WANTED

When Scott and Steve first conceived what the Beehive would look like, they pictured a café that was an eclectic mix of art, architecture and interior design. Scott, who minored in art while in college and took classes at the Pittsburgh Center for the Arts, knew that the look of the café would prove to be important as it attempted to create an image in the city.

In the original business plan, there is a section titled "Atmospheric." It is the longest section in the nearly sixty-page document. The partners felt it was important to describe the future look and feel of the café, including the type of furnishings selected, "Because so many of the physical elements of a room contribute greatly to the atmosphere," they wrote. Scott and Steve intended to create a "bohemian" atmosphere that they believed would attract a clientele who disregarded conventional standards of behavior and had artistic literary interests. The coffeehouse, they continued, would create a similar attitude through the manipulation of physical elements.

At first glance, the Beehive featured a haphazard collection of tables and chairs. It wasn't simply that the look and style differed from table to table, but the size and shape also varied. This might have seemed random, but like they did with much else in the coffeehouse, Scott and Steve had a plan.

The furniture was intended to resemble the "discarded charming furnishings found in a family's attic. The shop would convey a rustic, down-to-earth feeling." Unusual for furniture in cafés at the time, the Beehive's couches were intended to be placed in a smaller room that featured semi-dim lighting, adequate for reading but not harsh.

Mismatched furniture was the standard décor of the Beehive. *Photograph provided by Scott Kramer and Steve Zumoff.*

The pair already had designs that included plants, antique clocks, radios and other curiosities throughout the coffeehouse. Their designs for the walls and ceiling of the café included what they called "unconventional decorative techniques."

Scott had thoughts on how the art would be featured and hung in the space and even wanted it hung from the ceiling at odd angles. Unfortunately, an architect friend of Steve's advised against it. For the look of the walls, a simple decision was made.

"We put a sign up in the window that said, 'Artists Wanted," Scott remembered, "and people came out of the woodwork."

Perhaps understanding both the neighborhood and potential clientele, the Beehive's owners decided to tap the local market to see the reaction. Kramer said a stream of artists came in with portfolios, each excited about the possibility of having art exhibited at the café or the opportunity to paint its walls.

One of the first artists to talk with Scott and Steve was Kevin Schlosser, who painted a mural on the café's back wall that quickly became a favorite to many who visited the coffeehouse. The image of patrons swilling coffee with mugs in their hands remained from the day it was completed until the Beehive closed. In fact, so attached were the owners to the image that they

The mural painted before the Beehive opened that remained until the café was closed. *Photograph provided by Scott Kramer and Steve Zumoff.*

took the mural with them when they left, carefully removing the sections of drywall on which the image was painted.

Scott described watching one artist ply his trade. "On the way to the bathroom, he took some brown and painted a square, and then he took some yellow and added to that and painted another square. He added some red, painted another square. He only had a small amount of paint, but he did an entire wall. And then he painted a half-naked woman over it," he recalled.

In the bathroom, Scott remembered there were some Asian-inspired knickknacks, including plastic pagodas and wall hangings he had bought during the pair's trip to Toronto. He decided the men's room should be decorated to resemble a Chinese restaurant. They were so committed to the idea that the door used for the stall inside the bathroom was unlike those seen at most restaurants—it was an old refrigerator door. It was immediately filled with graffiti by artists and patrons when the café opened.

Mike Saxman painted a pagoda above the sink. Kramer called the artist brilliant and said he and Zumoff used him when they designed both the Lava Lounge and Tiki Lounge, two South Side bars opened by the pair several years later.

While the owners had ideas of the type of café they wanted, they were fairly lackadaisical in the direction they gave to the artists who worked on the space. "We had ideas; the artists had ideas," Zumoff said. "We let them do what they wanted, and it all kind of came together."

Although the artists were given free rein over what they painted, Scott said that he evaluated the work of the artists before deciding where their work would be featured. "If they had less talent," he said, "I put them in a less desirable spot."

Another local artist, Richard Bach, painted a dragon on the bathroom door. And while Bach's dragon was soon covered in graffiti, another contribution by the artist would forever be associated with the coffeehouse.

It was Bach and his partner, Pittsburgh artist Michael Lotenero, who created the iconic logo—a woman with a beehive in the middle of a yellow sun with the words

Beehive artwork created by Mike Saxman. *Scott Kramer and Steve Zumoff, private collection.*

36

"Beehive Coffee" surrounding her. The logo graced T-shirts, postcards, mugs and stickers and became immediately recognizable throughout the city.

Bach said that he had moved to the South Side shortly before the Beehive opened and was staying in an apartment on Fifteenth Street, later dubbed "Hellrose Place." The rent was less than $200 a month, a steal, even at 1990 Pittsburgh prices. Of course, the low rent required some compromises in living conditions. "There was a hole in the floor, and the basement looked like somebody had taken a TV repair correspondence course. There were all these 1970s-era TVs somewhat submerged in mud. But when the cops busted up a party, you could, at least, drop your drugs in the hole," he remembered.

Rick had met Lotenero at the Art Institute of Pittsburgh. The two graduated from the trade school and played together in various punk bands, usually started by Bach. They also founded the graphic design agency, 96 Eyes. Michael said the agency's name was taken from a lyric in the song "Human Fly" by the Cramps: "I got ninety-six tears and ninety-six eyes."

In their twenties, the partners spent the '90s creating a name for themselves. The agency won several ADDYs, awarded by the Pittsburgh Advertising Federation, during its lifespan, and both partners now have successful national and even international careers. Rick lives in Washington, D.C., and is represented by the Zynka Gallery in Sharpsburg. His industrial design work is featured at numerous locations, including the Mad Mex restaurant chain and the Smiling Moose locations. Mike's work has hung in museums, including the Carnegie Museum of Art, the Austin Museum of Digital Art, the Westmoreland Museum of Art, the Urban Institute of Contemporary Art-Michigan and the Mattress Factory.

While Rick and Mike are now both established in the commercial art world and command competitive pricing for their work, at the time, they were paid, like other artists who contributed work to the Beehive, in coffee. In lieu of money, which the Beehive didn't yet have, Steve said they gave out wooden tokens that could be exchanged for coffee. "Initially, when we opened, all the people that did art or work there were paid in coffee," he recalled. Those tokens became a point of pride for the early Beehive crowd—artists, baristas and customers who frequented the café in its nascent days—and are now often shown on Facebook groups and at infrequent get-togethers as proof of being part of the new scene. Rick remembered that he and Lotenero were given bags full of the tokens—they had so many, he sometimes traded them for beer.

Various logos created by 96 Eyes for coffee sold at the Beehive. *Scott Kramer and Steve Zumoff, private collection.*

Left: The front of Beehive tokens that were given to artists who painted the café. *David Rullo, private collection.*

Right: Many Beehive tokens. *Photograph provided by Scott Kramer and Steve Zumoff.*

The logo for the coffeehouse was truly a collaborative effort. Rick said Lotenero created the letters by hand, which was not an easy task since it was done without the use of computers.

Mike found the woman's face inside the sun and lettering from stacks of World War II–era *Life* magazines someone had given him that he kept as reference for graphic material. "I threw sunglasses and a beehive hairdo on her, put it in the middle of Mike's type and that was it," he recalled. "It was done."

Mike said that in addition to the logo, the pair created custom artwork on several of the tabletops, and Rick remembered that they created forty or fifty logos for custom roasted coffee flavors available at the coffeehouse. "Eventually, they ended up in *Print Magazine*'s Design Annual in the logo section in a two-page spread," Bach said.

The former drugstore's interior was lined with green and purple walls, orange ductwork and a ceiling painted like the sky. Original artwork was painted onto the coffeehouse's walls, doors and any other surface an artist might be able to reach, or it was hung, blurring the line between customer and designer.

Even the coffeehouse's first customer was influenced by the artists who helped create its ambience.

The first dollar made by the Beehive? *Scott Kramer and Steve Zumoff, private collection.*

Scott recalled that Tim Kaulen gave one of his tokens for free coffee to a homeless man immediately after the doors were unlocked for the first time. "He handed me the token and asked for a coffee. I told him he was our first customer. He got a big smile on his face, reached into his pocket and pulled out a crumbled dollar bill. He told me to hang it for good luck," Scott said.

Helping create the artwork and design gave those who shared their talents something they didn't have at other nightspots in the city: a sense of ownership. No, they didn't select the coffee, pay the rent or settle the bills with vendors, but they were part of the aesthetics, further tying them to the coffeehouse. It also helped to develop a scene in the early days of the café. Because of this, there was no need to work at creating an identity for the coffeehouse, as the artists who had labored on the look had already given it one.

That identity would be further locked down by the slingers who poured the coffee, prepared the espresso and cappuccinos, distributed the cakes and sweets and worked the registers.

3

"YOU HAVE A JOB WORKING AT THE BEEHIVE"

Valerie Gatchell-Christofel is often remembered for her tattoo. A looped line of figures on her upper arm, it was frequently visible when she worked as a barista, or coffee slinger, as they were known, at the Beehive. It was also shared with one of Generation X's most famous bass players: Flea (but more on that later).

The Ohio transplant started working at the café several months after it opened. An Art Institute graduate who had been living on the North Side, Gatchell-Christofel moved across town to be closer to the action. The Beehive had just opened, but the nonstop activity and constant flow of people made her curious. "I remember sitting on the corner for the first week watching people go in, and I was like, 'This is so New York City. This is so cool.' Just watching all these neat people walk in, I was like, 'I have to get a job there.'"

Getting hired at the new coffeehouse, however, proved to be more of a challenge than Valerie had anticipated. She spent a month lobbying the manager daily. "I begged every single day for a job. She hated me because I had this squeaky high voice. Eventually though, she hired me, and we became good friends. She was in my first wedding, and we're still friends to this day."

Having recently graduated from the Art Institute, wearing the same fashion, listening to the same alternative music and living in the same neighborhood as many of those who patronized the coffeehouse, Valerie was the perfect example of the type of barista hired by Kramer and Zumoff. There existed no distinction between customer and employee. In fact, most

It's A SURPRISE BASH for our gal VAL Thurs. 3·19·92 @ 9:30 pm @ THE HIVE where else?

The Beehive was known to host a party or two. *Photograph provided by Valerie Gatchell-Christofel.*

employees were customers first, so enamored with the Beehive that they went home as little as possible and figured they might as well get paid for pouring coffee or cleaning up after hours.

For Valerie, the allure of the coffeehouse was more than the work of brewing espresso and cutting cake. The employees, she said, were like supermodels, on display for the customers. The café was a scene maker, especially in its early days, when people came in to hear what music was playing or what clothes were worn by the baristas. "It hit me," she said. "I would come here and hang out and drink coffee all day and watch them, and now, I'm going to be one of them. It was about so much more than just making coffee back then."

To prepare for her debut, Valerie went shopping. The former fashion merchandising major did what most Gen Xers were doing at the time: she went to the Red White and Blue, a large thrift store in the city. There, bought what she called "her uniform": Doc Marten boots, fishnet stockings, cutoff blue denim shorts, a baggy white V-neck T-shirt and a flannel shirt.

Having the right look didn't prevent Valerie from experiencing first-day jitters. "My very first night, I was so nervous that I sliced the piece of cake with a knife upside down. [I] was like, 'Oh, my God. I wasn't even paying attention to the knife blade,'" she remembered.

As a new employee, Valerie worked hard to learn the Beehive's system, which included not only how to cut cakes but also how to efficiently unload the dishwasher. "At home, you took two coffee mugs and you put them away and came back for more. At the Beehive, we were so busy, and we needed those mugs. They were always calling for more. I learned the first night to put one on this finger and one on this finger and to hold another with each hand and then put one in between so there were seven coffee mugs."

JEN SAFFRON HAD RECENTLY graduated with an arts degree from Carnegie Mellon University and thought to herself, "I need a fucking break. I just worked my ass of for four years, and I'm tired."

The budding photographer knew that the South Side had a developing art scene through her involvement with the Silver Eye Center for Photography, located on East Carson Street. She said she first heard of the Beehive from friends. "I went there, and I was just blown away by how fun it was. The art, the artistry, the music. I thought, 'You know what, I would work at a place like this,'" she said.

Saffron, who had worked in food service while in school, remembered receiving a large book about coffee to read on her first day working at the café, which explained the different types of beans and where they grow—something she said she had never thought about before being hired by the Beehive.

Her salary was $4.25 an hour plus tips. "I think minimum wage was $4.10 at the time, so it was a little more than that."

When she started, Jen said, the South Side hadn't yet strayed very far from its immigrant roots. Next to the Beehive, she recalled, was the Windmill Deli, which sold potato salad sandwiches. There were other delis and poultry places and an active Serbian club, the future business owner said.

The new café brushed up and against this community, which wasn't always comfortable with the changes taking place in their neighborhood. "Our presence there was welcomed by a group of people that were planting a flag on the South Side as a place to do their art and make stuff happen," she said. Others weren't so happy. As an example, she cited those who would come in wanting a cup of coffee for the

By 1993, a handbook had been created for Beehive employees. *Scott Kramer and Steve Zumoff, private collection.*

price they were used to paying at the delis and diners around town. These people, Saffron remembered, bristled at the eighty-cent cost of the coffee. "They would say, 'This is outrageous.' They were scandalized," she said.

Jen worked the night shift, and despite the community that was developing in the coffeehouse, she remembered that sometimes, things could get tense depending on who came into the café, especially as the bars began to close. She remembered one moment when a biker came in wearing a motorcycle helmet with a swastika painted on it. "I was like, 'Get the fuck out of here.' And he was like, 'What are you saying to me?' And I was like, 'I said, get the fuck out.' You know, especially since Scott and Steve were Jewish."

Like Valerie, Saffron, too, learned a lot of new information while working at the Beehive—for instance, cheesecake, if left out, would absorb cigarette smoke.

Coming from the straight-edged world of Carnegie Mellon, Jen said she hadn't been exposed to people who would steal from where they worked, something that occurred while she was employed at the coffeehouse. "I was horrified, but most of the people that worked there did so because they had to, so they stole out of desperation," she said.

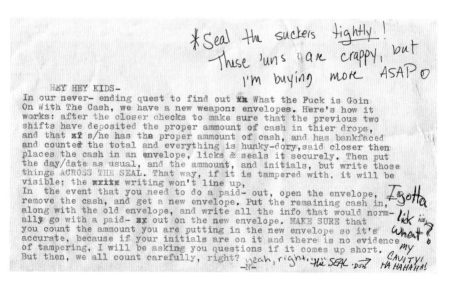

Above: Scott and Steve believed they came up with a solution to missing cash issues at the coffeehouse. The employees, as you can see by the handwritten notes, weren't so sure. *Scott Kramer and Steve Zumoff, private collection.*

Opposite: The Beehive had Pride long before it was fashionable. *Scott Kramer and Steve Zumoff, private collection.*

Jen eventually moved to the day shift, noting the change in customers. The daylight hours were filled with artists who didn't have jobs to go to, so they would spend all day at the café, nursing their coffee and discussing projects.

Of course, not everyone who visited the café had such high goals as creating art. "One day I came to work, and Val was having a conniption because a river rat had crawled through the sewer and was dead in the toilet," she said. "I was like, 'There's not a chance in hell that I'm going to be taking care of that.'" It did give her the idea for a joke, however. Jen made a cardboard mouse that she would place around the store, something she said Scott didn't find very funny.

What the Beehive created, she offered, was a place with a sense of belonging for the scrappy crowd who frequented it. "It felt like home," she said. "It was unmistakable."

ANDREW LASSWELL WAS SLIGHTLY younger than many of the Beehive's other patrons when he discovered the coffeehouse in April 1991. He and his friend skipped their afternoon classes at Pittsburgh Creative and Performing Arts School (CAPA), Pittsburgh's magnet high school focused on art. "We decided to go check out this weird coffeehouse," he said. "I remember we played checkers, drank tea and sat in one of the side tables."

Andrew said that after dropping out of high school, he spent most of his time "loafing" at the Beehive. It was after a move to the nearby community on Mount Washington that he began working at the café. "My roommate came home and told me I had a job cleaning floors," he remembered.

Initially, he worked at the Beehive's Oakland location before working as a janitor both there and the South Side café. He later joined the ranks of the coffee slingers in 1993. He stayed in that position until 1996.

Andrew's experience was not unique. The boundary between customer and employee often blurred. It was a regular occurrence for a patron to become a slinger before playing at the café in a band. If they happened to need a job again, Scott and Steve would often hire them back.

This was the case for Valerie, who would often spend extended periods away from the coffeehouse during her tenure working there, as she was often in New York or California, employed in the fashion and entertainment industries. "I was trying to be a makeup artist in Manhattan, so I was going to New York, traveling a lot to L.A., but every single time I came back to Pittsburgh, Steve and Scott gave me my job back," she recalled. "I could leave for a week, and they would be fine; leave for two weeks, and they would be fine. They always let me come back to work."

That experience was shared by David Gruen, who worked as a janitor at the café. After returning from an extended trip he took to California with a girlfriend, he met Scott on the street, who asked, "Are you still working for me?"

MANNING THE SHIP FOR Scott and Steve, Marla Louis Misch was the first manager of the South Side location.

The former Chicagoan had an attractive skillset that made her indispensable to the owners—she had an intimate knowledge of Starbucks and its menu. The chain hadn't spread east yet but had four locations in the Windy City. Scott and Steve had visited one of the locations on their cross-country trip to see the Jerry Garcia band and decided that when they opened a coffeehouse, the menu would be perfect.

The arrival of Misch, who was living on the South Side somewhere between Thirteenth and Eighteenth Streets near the river, eliminated the need for the two to make numerous trips to the city or hire an industrial spy. Instead, they simply leaned into her knowledge of how each drink was made. "They didn't really know coffee," Marla said, noting that the drink ideas in the early days of the Beehive came from her.

What the duo did have, she said, was a notebook filled with ideas. "One was just cats," she remembered. "They wanted

Marla Misch arguing with a police officer during South Side Street Spectacular. "Don't you feel silly the way you are dressed?" Marla said the officer asked her. "Don't you?" she replied. *Photograph provided by Marla Misch.*

If you didn't want to tip your slinger, how about you tip their cat? *Scott Kramer and Steve Zumoff, private collection.*

cats to hang out there. Nowadays, maybe that would work, but in the '90s, cats in restaurants was not a big thing."

It was also Marla who formalized the inner workings of the Beehive in its initial stages. She worked with Steve and Scott behind the counter but said that after two weeks, the café was making so much money that she took them off the schedule and began hiring employees. She also developed the stations where each employee worked, creating a system that would, in theory, guarantee smooth service.

Marla found the first group of slingers through local bands she was in and people she met in the local music scene. "I ended up hiring as many freaky people as I could. They were all very dependable. I only had to fire one person during my time there, and I can't remember her name," she said.

Marla, who grew up in West Virginia and attended college there before moving to Chicago, said that the Beehive opened her up to new experiences. "There was a customer who invited me to see the Ms. Pennsylvania contest. I said, 'Yeah, that sounds like fun.' They were the prettiest men I had ever seen. It was the *Miss* Pennsylvania contest; it was all drag queens. It was downtown in an old building that had been converted into a gay club," she remembered.

SCOTT AND STEVE MIGHT not have known much about coffee before opening the Beehive, but they quickly became aficionados. More than that, though, they were entrepreneurs with a vision.

Theo Logos was, at turns, a customer, writer, musician and employee at the coffeehouse. The Mount Pleasant native had returned to the Steel City after traveling around the country for a period.

He remembered Kramer as a man who was unafraid to try different ideas, knowing that they wouldn't all work. "Some of them were just completely off the wall and people would laugh at it, but I said, 'This is what idea people do. Yes, he has ten dumb ideas, but then he comes up with one great idea.'

An idea moment with Scott? *Photograph provided by Scott Kramer and Steve Zumoff.*

He was always throwing stuff on the wall to see what stuck," he said. "I had real respect for that."

On the other hand, Theo said that an idea man sometimes needed a foil to operate a successful business, a role Steve proved more than adept at handling. "Scott knew how to come up with ideas, but Steve was practical. Steve knew how to make stuff happen," he said.

Theo said that, often, it's not the employees who are inundated with the day-to-day details of a business who recognize the need for an idea person. "I always had a lot of respect for them, probably more than some of their regular employees," he noted.

Marla was already the manager when Natalie Gilchrist was hired as a coffee slinger at the new café.

A graduate from Indiana University of Pennsylvania, Natalie was living in another Pittsburgh neighborhood, Polish Hill, but worked at Kinkos near the Beehive. She said it was during one of Steve's trips to the store that the two started a conversation and he asked her if she wanted a job.

Natalie said that she was probably the second employee at the coffeehouse and that she usually worked the early morning shift, Monday through Friday, beginning at 7:00 a.m. "Steve and Scott had a vision of what they wanted the place to be like, which was cool because it totally fit into my aesthetic," she remembered.

Kramer, she recalled, would often arrive at the café early in her shift and double check that menial tasks like sweeping the sidewalk had been completed before the space started to fill, usually around 10:00 a.m. He would then come behind the counter—something discouraged by the slingers. "Steve would come in and do the paychecks and just kind of walk behind the counter to make sure things were clean and in good working order, and then he was gone," Valerie remembered. "Scott would come in and try to be behind the coffee and do the coffee, and we were like, 'You can go mingle with the people. You can't be back here.'"

And while the café itself had a laid-back atmosphere and many of the employees spoke of the laissez-faire attitude that often helped them form long-lasting friendships with the owners, managers and customers, Natalie said there were times when Scott and Steve sometimes engaged in tactics that were far more corporate than their reputations let on.

Natalie remembered that she often received large tips during her shift, prompting Scott to spend one day working with her to see how she did it. Gilchrist said she believed he thought she was stealing the tips. But it was another occurrence that led to her leave the café.

The owners hired secret shoppers to frequent the coffeehouse and report their findings. "I was working behind the counter, and one of my coworkers came in," she remembered. "He had a roommate that came in with him." Natalie said that one of the perks that came with working at the

Nikole wasn't only a Beehive employee, she was a customer, too. *Photograph provided by Nikole Boyda McGuiness.*

Valerie Gatchell-Christofel and her mother, Beehive employee Judy Dickson. *Photograph provided by Scott Kramer and Steve Zumoff.*

Beehive was receiving free drinks and half-priced food. Her coworker gave his roommate his free coffee and a donut. The private investigators who were working for Scott and Steve reported that Gilchrist *and* her coworker had provided free food. For this, Natalie had the distinction of being the one person Marla ever fired. "Marla read me everything the private investigators said, and I was like, 'I guess they're really serious. They don't want me to work here anymore.'"

Natalie looks back at the incident as a positive, feeling she was already stretched working multiple jobs. The decision by Scott and Steve allowed her to focus on her graphic design career. In fact, despite no longer being employed at the Beehive, Natalie said she continued to help the owners by coming up with a quick flyer or assisting them with their other needs. "I still love those guys," she said. "I'm not knocking them."

Many of the Beehive's employees have warm memories of their time there. Valerie enjoyed working there so much, she said, that when her mother was looking to move from Florida to Pittsburgh, she secured her a job at the café. "I told her I can't come to Pittsburgh unless I have job," Valerie's mother, Judy Dickson, recalled. "She said, 'Well, you have a job working at the Beehive.' That was my first job." Dickson said she worked at the coffeehouse as a janitor for just under a year, and despite her short tenure there, she credits the Beehive with helping her find community—something she's thankful for thirty years later. "That's how I got to know everyone," she said, "because absolutely everyone congregated at the Beehive."

As IMPORTANT AS THE slingers were to both the operations and culture of the Beehive were the janitors. The revolving cast of characters included frequent customers, friends who needed jobs, musicians, artists and other residents from the neighborhood.

Aside from Dickson, other notable janitors included Phat Man Dee, Rusted Root's Michael Glabicki and Circus Apocalypse's David Gruen.

Gruen recalled in an interview that was recorded during the coffeehouse's final week for the Heinz History Center that the term *JoA* was coined for the maintenance workers. The term stood for "janitors on acid," and it was created because it was believed that at one time, every janitor had cleaned the café on the hallucinogenic.

Michael Glabicki was hired by Bob Ziller, a Beehive employee who worked in several different roles during his time at the coffeehouse. Remarkably, it was after Rusted Root had already started to gain national

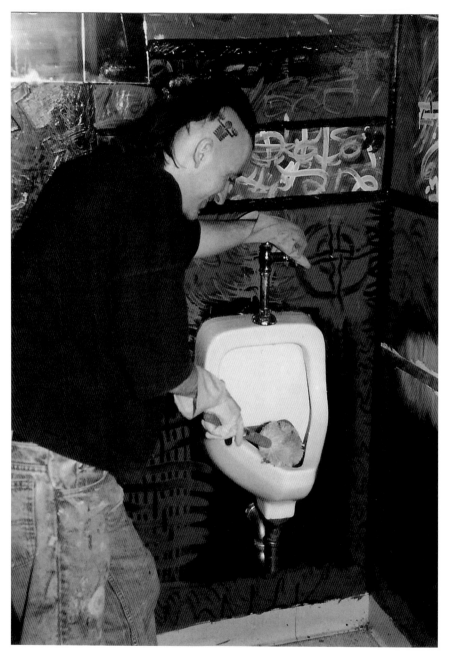

Cleaning the Beehive was a thankless job. *Photograph provided by Scott Kramer and Steve Zumoff.*

attention. Bob said that the singer and guitarist simply wanted a job he could perform during his downtime from touring. He hoped the role would help him stay "rooted."

Glabicki, Bob noted, was able to gain perspective after only a few weeks.

Both Damon Griffith and his wife, Sabrina, worked as janitors. Sabrina moved to Pittsburgh after completing art school. She met Damon and, within a week of living in the city, fell madly in love and applied for a job at the coffeehouse. "Being a Beehive janitor was a prestigious job," she said. "I was a janitor the entire time I lived in Pittsburgh." Damon, too, spent time working as a janitor, saying he spent several stints in the role. Each time, he remembered, Scott would fire him. "Getting fired by Scott was a mark of distinction," Sabrina said (one she noted she never earned).

LIKE JEN, MARK HANNEMAN moved to Pittsburgh after studying at Indiana University of Pennsylvania. "There was a whole exodus out of Indiana and IUP to Oakland and the South Side of really talented, intelligent people," he said.

Mark eventually ended up staying at Hellrose Place on Fifteenth Street and worked as a janitor with Damon and Andrew. It was the future light designer who gave the apartment, which would be home to many in the Beehive's circle, its name, taken in part from *Melrose Place*, the popular show about a group of rich, young white students living in California. Hellrose Place would share none of the television show's traits.

Mark's time at the coffeehouse was sometimes motivated by where he was staying, and as a resident of Hellrose Place, he said the Beehive offered a much safer and more sanitary option for food. "I couldn't step foot in the kitchen [at Hellrose Place], because there was like a split [in] the floor, and it was going to fall into the building," he said. "It was dangerous to cook, and I wasn't OK with that."

Hanneman also worked as part of the coffeehouse's cleaning crew. He said while those who cleaned the café were amorphous, he would sometimes work a shift. Other times, Laswell or Phat Man Dee might have worked janitorial a shift. And still, the job was sometimes done by someone who was not even hired as a janitor.

Hanneman recounted in an interview that was recorded during the Beehive's final week celebration that he bartered with local teens and allowed them to spend nights in the café in exchange for cleaning it. The agreement was terminated after Steve returned unexpectedly one night to the café, where Mark was working on a theater lighting project, designs stretched across the tabletops, as the teens cleaned the Beehive.

Given the lackadaisical attitude of the cleaning crew, it shouldn't come as a shock to learn that, at times, the janitors were less than rigorous about their assigned tasks.

Phat Man Dee said that she would sometimes sleep under the pinball machines that were in the café, dreaming she had already finished her cleaning. "And then I would wake up next to cigarette butts and little ash mountains," she said.

At one point, someone threw up shortly before opening, and the janitors didn't properly clean it. Man Dee remembered owner Steve Zumoff saying, "I know you aren't on the clock, but can you at least get the chunks?" From that point forward, the creed "can you just get the chunks?" became a popular refrain among the janitors.

GEORGE ANDREWS WAS AN early employee as well, but he wasn't employed as a coffee slinger or janitor. He booked the bands that played in the South Side location during the café's early days.

He had recently returned to Pittsburgh after taking a yearlong sabbatical from his job as an art teacher at the Western Pennsylvania School. The future owner of the East Carson Street staple the Culture Shop spent the year traveling throughout India, Nepal and Thailand. When he returned from his trip to Southeastern Asia, Andrews discovered that the job he thought was waiting for him had been eliminated. "Suddenly, I had no job and was collecting unemployment. At some point, I moved to the South Side and got a job at the Beehive. I talked my way into booking music there," he recalled.

In actuality, Andrews had met Scott in Oakland, where the School of the Blind was located and where Kramer hung out with Steve. He told him of his plans to open the coffeehouse. George thought it was an interesting idea, since Pittsburgh didn't yet have any trendy coffeehouses, but he didn't think much else about it until he returned to the South Side and began seeking gainful employment.

"We would have music five days a week," Andrews said. "They had an OK speaker system, and I booked mostly acoustic-type acts."

George said he started to work behind the counter, too, one of the many slingers. Like Valerie, he remembered there being a large collection of people who served coffee and cut desserts.

Eventually, George parlayed the gig into a management role.

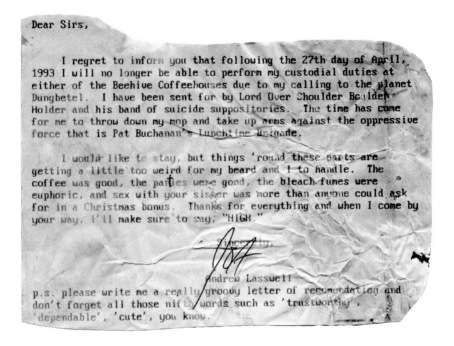

Dear Sirs,

     I regret to inform you that following the 27th day of April, 1993 I will no longer be able to perform my custodial duties at either of the Beehive Coffeehouses due to my calling to the planet Dungbetel. I have been sent for by Lord Over Shoulder Boulder Holder and his band of suicide suppositories. The time has come for me to throw down my mop and take up arms against the oppressive force that is Pat Buchanan's Lunchtime Brigade.

     I would like to stay, but things 'round these parts are getting a little too weird for my beard and I to handle. The coffee was good, the parties were good, the bleach fumes were euphoric, and sex with your sister was more than anyone could ask for in a Christmas bonus. Thanks for everything and when I come by your way, I'll make sure to say, "HIGH."

                   Sincerely,

                   Andrew Lasswell

p.s. please write me a really groovy letter of recommendation and don't forget all those nifty words such as 'trustworthy', 'dependable', 'cute', you know.

Andrew Laswell's resignation letter. *Scott Kramer and Steve Zumoff, private collection.*

"There were many people behind the counter and several managers. They were still trying to figure it out. The employees were there trying to make business happen, and I was there trying to book music, and Steve was there trying to make things work, and Scott had these ideas about the décor, finding secondhand items. It was really revolutionary for its time for the South Side. We didn't have a coffee shop. It was immediately a hit," Andrews said.

The South Side, George said, "became a very cool place to be."

And while that coolness factor wasn't only due to the Beehive, it was certainly one of the original progenitors of the area's reputation and personality.

Like it was in any hip period, the accompanying soundtrack was critical.

4

THE MUSIC

If caffeine and chocolate were the fire that fueled the Beehive, music was the defining touchstone for many who frequented the café. It isn't surprising that music played such a central role, given the importance of the Grateful Dead to Scott and Steve's relationship.

Generation X, named after Douglas Coupland's first novel, shook off the classic rock of their parents and embraced a new style of music created by their contemporaries: alternative rock. The genre comprised everything from college rock bands like the Replacements and R.E.M. to goth artists, including Peter Murphy and the Cure, and industrial acts like Ministry and Skinny Puppy.

All of those styles, however, were dwarfed by a new genre of heavy rock that, like the coffeehouse scene the Beehive was a part of, came from Seattle: grunge. Part punk, part heavy metal and part sludge, grunge soon became the de facto listening choice of teens and young adults across the country and the world.

MTV featured bands like Alice in Chains, Mudhoney, Pearl Jam, Soundgarden and the omnipresent Nirvana on a twenty-four-hour loop. Pittsburgh was soon home to two alternative FM rock channels, WXDX and WNRQ, as well as several college radio stations that featured the music format and appealed to the new generation just beginning to find its way.

These new rock stars were the same age as the Beehive's customers and looked similar: Doc Martens, ripped jeans, flannel shirts, jackets bought from thrift stores, T-shirts with ironic logos and the names of obscure rock

A Battle of the Bands flyer at the Oakland Beehive. *Scott Kramer and Steve Zumoff, private collection.*

bands. Perhaps more importantly, the artists in the band shared the same disaffected outlook as their fans.

Pittsburgh had its own music scene. It was not quite as heavy, influenced more by the jam scene and hippie outlook of the previous generation. Bands including Rusted Root and Psoas played the same clubs as the heavier

Kelly Affair and electronic Mace, but they could also find a comfortable perch playing in some of the jam-based festivals that were beginning to become popular.

Many of these bands both played at the coffeehouse and used it as a meeting space. In fact, at least one future rock star, Kyp Malone of TV on the Radio, slept in the crawl space above the bathroom before he moved to New York and gained a foothold in the music industry.

The largest and most popular neo-hippie band of the day, Rusted Root, had one of its earliest gigs at the Beehive and used the coffeehouse as a meeting place before it signed a deal with Mercury Records, part of the Universal Music Group.

A Beehive bathroom. *Photograph by David Grim.*

Former Rusted Root band member Jenn Wertz started going to the café shortly after it opened. She had recently moved back to Pittsburgh from Los Angeles with her boyfriend. They rented an apartment on the corner of Fourteenth and East Carson Streets, central to the developing art scene in the neighborhood and near the coffeehouse.

After a brief stint at the Art Institute of Pittsburgh, Wertz dropped out and began trying to figure out what she would do next. The Beehive was the place where she spent much of her days. Not yet twenty-one, Wertz said the Beehive offered a place for her to drink café mochas, use the pay phone (a carryover from the pharmacy that previously occupied the space), smoke and be near people playing guitar or drawing customers. The fact that it was open twenty-four hours was a plus.

Wertz's boyfriend worked at Triangle Messenger Service, one of two bike messenger companies that operated in the city at the time; it was a popular form of delivery memorialized in *Quicksilver*, a movie starring Kevin Bacon. "The core group of people that hung out at the Beehive at the start were bike messengers and musicians," she remembered. Bolstering Wertz's claim, Brian Rose followed what he called "the pure Pittsburgh trajectory." "I worked at the Beehive, and then I became a bicycle messenger. I spent

A deck of cards with the Beehive logo. *Scott Kramer and Steve Zumoff, private collection.*

from the age of nineteen or twenty until the age of thirty-eight working in the bicycle industry," he said.

The South Side, Wertz said, was still postindustrial and destitute and didn't offer a lot of creative opportunities when the bike messengers and first-generation artists could still find cheap rent and substandard homes along East Carson Street. "There were old men who were displaced and drunk, walking down the streets going from Dee's to the Black Onyx to the Birmingham Inn. They were old steel workers," she said. The neighborhood, Wertz recalled, was shadowed, figuratively and literally, by abandoned steel mills.

Wertz and her boyfriend John Buyak eventually went to see Rusted Root at the Upstage, a popular Oakland bar that would come to be known for its DJs, goth- and '80s-themed nights and twenty-five-cent drafts.

Buyak is a multi-instrumentalist who was eventually offered a place in Rusted Root by its founder, Mike Glabicki. Surprisingly, he also asked Wertz to join. "I was like, 'I'm not a musician.' And he said, 'Oh, you will be. Trust me,'" she remembered. "That's a really wonderful gift he gave me."

The coffeehouse became a place for the band to meet when they weren't rehearsing or playing gigs, she said. "It was our meeting place, and if they had an event, like their one-year anniversary, we would come and play," she said, noting that the performance has become part of local South Side lore. It was captured on video, has been uploaded to YouTube and includes the Beehive's original cast of characters.

Fellow band member Liz Berlin said she remembered seeing coffeehouses from time to time as she toured the country in the nascent days of Rusted Root. "But they would only be in the hippest of places—New York City or Denver, Colorado," she said. "I heard about this new place in Pittsburgh, where they didn't serve alcohol and you could buy coffee and other things, too. It was more like a central place for artists and free thinkers that could go and hang out there for hours." Having the Beehive in the city was valuable, she said, because it provided a place for creatives of different disciplines to hang out and talk and collaborate.

Liz had met Glabicki in high school, before Scott and Steve opened the coffeehouse, and was already playing music with him at the time. Michael was the chief songwriter in the band, and Liz helped fine tune his ideas while working on her own music.

And while the band didn't form at the Beehive, Liz said it was a place where they all hung out.

Once Rusted Root found success, Liz said that the café offered a place that felt like home when she returned from touring.

The back room also provided the band a place to play, and the Oakland location delivered some of Berlin's favorite memories of gigging in the city. "The shows there were really special," she remembered. "We would take over the whole theater and set up the drums and everything. During

Rusted Root playing at the Oakland Beehive. *Sketch by Bill Patterson, taken from* Pit Stop for the Angels, *published by Lascaux Editions; used with permission.*

soundcheck, we would spread the drums all throughout the audience and have drum jams with everybody playing. It was really just great synergy of people and energy."

Several years later, after leaving Rusted Root, Liz went on to create Mr. Smalls Theater, a musical venue in Millvale, Pennsylvania. The former church includes a recording studio, several performance spaces, an artist development not-for-profit and a restaurant/coffee shop that is, at least, Beehive inspired.

GREG FELMLEY LIVED ON the South Side, supporting himself as a bike messenger in the early days of Psoas, a Pittsburgh-based band in which he played acoustic guitar and sang. "I had to be a bicycle messenger just to afford ramen noodles," he said.

The Beehive, he noted, was a hub for musicians and other artists. "It was our salon. We were all musicians in bands. Even Rusted Root, who, by that point, were too big to play there, hung out there," he said.

Musicians, including Greg Felmley, performing at the Beehive. *Photograph provided by Scott Kramer and Steve Zumoff.*

Greg's neo-hippie band wasn't as big as Rusted Root, but it found a loyal audience in the city. In fact, the band's fans included actor Woody Harrelson and his brother Brett. Psoas was playing a show on the local National Public Radio affiliate WYEP when Harrelson called in to say he liked what he heard and was interested in hanging out with the musicians. Wary that the call was placed by friends rather than the actor who had made his name on the sitcom *Cheers*, the band said they couldn't speak to whoever was on the other end of the line and hung up. Harrelson, who was in town to film the movie *Kingpin*, called back, convinced the band that he was in fact the actor and invited them to play at a party he and his brother were throwing. The actor eventually offered to help the band produce a CD. The resultant recording, *Blood Flow*, was released on Onoma Record, then home to the Gathering Field, another popular Pittsburgh band.

Local jazz musician, Beehive employee, artist and curio Phat Man Dee was a constant presence at the coffeehouse. From attending screenings of *The Rocky Horror Picture Show* as a high school student at the Oakland location to working as a janitor and taking part in some of the more famous— and infamous—escapades at the café, Mandy Kivowitz-Delfaver became, to many, synonymous with the cafe. Phat Man Dee was so linked to the Beehive that when she married her husband, Tommy Amoeba, the wedding occurred on East Carson Street, was attended by thousands and included a stop at the coffeehouse.

Man Dee had studied music since she was eight or nine years old and said she was enrolled in the Pittsburgh Center for the Musically Talented, a Saturday program. It was her intention to become either a musician or a lawyer, something that never came to fruition after she decided to devote her energies to the arts.

The singer said that she spent most of her high school days hanging out at the Beehive's Oakland location because she didn't have a car and it was where most of her friends went. Only after she dropped out of college did she begin spending her days at the South Side coffeehouse.

Both locations, she said, proved crucial in her development as a musician. "Scott and Steve let me put together a show with my first jazz band in the lobby of the Oakland Beehive. It didn't really work out, but they let me try. I booked my first big show in the theater and smaller shows in the Lava Lounge [another club Kramer and Zumoff eventually opened on East Carson Street], where I played every Monday night," she said.

While she was learning her craft and finding her voice as an artist, Man Dee was also producing concerts at the coffeehouse. She said these tended to be variety shows that featured musicians, poets, drag queens, belly dancers, comedians and other nontraditional acts. "I loved that I could put together whatever I wanted," she said. "Nobody ever made any money. I think they gave me a small budget, but that went to the performers."

LIAM JOHN IS A member of the band the Quiet Loud. The band has supported several artists, including post-grunge band Sponge. Liam is also one of the founders of Wake Up on Fire Records.

Liam was originally known as Johnny St. Lethal and said that the Beehive provided a source of inspiration as he created what was originally a booking agency for bands before it morphed into a development company for musicians. "We knew we weren't going to last as a booking agent, so the question became: How could we best help artists?" he said.

Liam said that for many bands, the ability to learn how to become more than "Pittsburgh famous," is daunting. He decided a new paradigm was needed from the way most record labels work. Instead of signing a band and rushing them out before they've honed their skills, Wake Up on Fire

The Beehive developed the mold for Pittsburgh acoustic artists to play at coffeehouses. *Photograph provided by Scott Kramer and Steve Zumoff.*

is more interested in helping artists develop long-term skills. "We decided we'll charge a nominal fee for a retainer, and then every week, we'll help them develop. We'll come to rehearsals, help with their songs and get them nationally competitive ready," he said. The next move is to transition to into a record label, he said, releasing physical products.

Liam discovered the Beehive with his cousins, he said, noting that it provided him the opportunity to make mistakes and mature as a person and artist. "It was just this magic space that Steve and Scott created," he said. "I don't think they grasp the impact and how much that did for so many people."

OF COURSE, NOT ALL the musicians associated with the Beehive were members of Gen X. Take eighty-year-old Chuck Owston for example. The guitarist and pastor from North Versailles was visiting one of his parishioners at Mercy Hospital when someone told him about a new coffeehouse on the South Side. "A beatnik place they said," he remembered. "I said, 'Well, I've never been to the South Side. The first time I went, I saw a girl with purple hair. I had never seen that before." Less than a year later, Owston traveled to England to see the Fairport Convention and said many in the crowd had multicolored hair, but it would take another six months before it was more than a rarity in Pittsburgh.

Owston moved to the South Side for a time in the '90s. He played in various shows and bands during this time at the café, including one called the Cigar Box Riffraff. "It was all homeless guys except me and Cathy Hickling," he remembered.

He performed with another Beehive customer in a band known as Catfish Row. "He played the washboard, and I played the cigar box guitar," he said.

Owston has performed everything from Americana to blues to Victorian, gothic and metal music, and on more than one occasion, he's played as the member of a jug band, often with people he first met at the Beehive.

The musician was frequently several generations older than most of the people who came to the coffeehouse. "I had a girlfriend that said to me, 'What do you see in these people?' I told her, 'I see potential creativity.'"

Numerous other bands started and played at the Beehive, as well. The basement of the South Side location was a performance space for a short period, as were an upstairs room and the movie theater at the Oakland location.

A short list of notable local bands included artist Rick Bach, who was in several musical projects, including the Cavemen from Oklahoma. Beehive janitor, art curator and gallery owner Bob Ziller started Bingo Quixote. And 210 included Beehive regular Brian Cummings.

SOME OF THE BANDS that had a connection to the Beehive were more well-known across the country.

The Red Hot Chili Peppers spent most of the '90s as one of the biggest alternative bands not to hail from Seattle. The four-piece band even headlined Lollapalooza 2, the first time the alternative festival toured the country. It was a Gen X touchstone, featuring a lineup that included not only the Chili Peppers but also Soundgarden, Pearl Jam, Ministry and the Jesus and Mary Chain, and it was of interest to many of the Beehive's customers.

Xavier Evan Carraher, a frequent Beehive customer and local artist, remembered the Red Hot Chili Peppers hanging out at the Beehive after a show. "They came and just hung out in the big booth for a good half hour without anyone noticing or caring," Xavier said. "When people did notice, they would just walk by and say, 'Good job, guys.'" The Peppers enjoyed the anonymity the coffeehouse provided before it was broken. "One younger

person, younger than all of us, was like, 'Wait a minute, do you know who's here?' They got up and left. Everyone was like, 'You suck,' because they were just having a great time being unnoticed and absorbing the vibe."

The connection between the coffeehouse and the rock band was more than skin deep for at least one of the Beehive regulars and employees.

Valerie Gatchel-Christofel, who spent time on the road with the Smashing Pumpkins, Janes Addiction, Pearl Jam and the Red Hot Chili Peppers is often remembered for the tattoo she has around her arm. The design is one she saw in the apartment of a friend. "He had these drawings of stick people, and I was like, 'That would be such a cute tattoo.' He was like, 'That's stupid,' so I stole it and had them tattooed on my arm."

Fast forward a few years, and Valerie had moved to Los Angeles, California, and was hanging out at a bar with friends. "Flea from the Red Hot Chili Peppers started pushing people out of the way to get to me. He was like, 'That's my tattoo,' and I was like, 'Yeah, whatever.' And he said, 'No, I drew that.'" The next day, the bass player visited the Pittsburgh transplant at the coffeehouse, where she was working, and showed her the band's new CD. Sure enough, the image adorning her arm was included in the artwork.

The Jesus Lizard was another punk band with a connection to the coffeehouse. The band played at the Oakland location. David Grim, who worked and had his photography displayed at the Beehive, remembered the show for the events that took place off the stage. "There was this doorman, Mark Choi [a manager at the Oakland location], who was a smart guy but probably on the spectrum. He was a black belt and was running around the show in these tiny whities. The show was crazy, and he was just all over the place, and I remember the singer tackled him, which was really interesting."

SO IMPORTANT TO THE Beehive was the music and culture built around it that owner Steve Zumoff remembered the shop serving as a gathering place the day Kurt Cobain died. "Everyone just started showing up," he said. "It was like a wake."

Music would come to play a large role in revitalizing the South Side. Clubs, including Nick's Fat City, Club Café and the Rex Theater, would help the neighborhood establish itself as a home for local and national bands and touring acts.

As important as music was to the Beehive and the community, art played as large a role in establishing the South Side's identity.

5

A MUSICAL INTERLUDE

BLUE DUCK RECORDS

E very nascent music scene needs a record label that helps define it. For Seattle, that was Sub Pop; in Chicago, Wax Trax nursed the industrial and heavy dance culture; punk was the sound of Long Beach's SST Records. In Pittsburgh, there was Blue Duck Records.

Created by Bree Freeman in 1992, Blue Duck Records was about as far as you could get from Pittsburgh's previous rock output. Blue-collar artists like Joe Grushecky and Donnie Iris had little in common with the alternative music popular with much of Generation X, a large portion of which fell into genres like grunge and industrial. A strong acoustic/coffeehouse ethos was also developing.

Many of these bands found a home on Blue Duck Records and its compilation discs—*Duck Tracks*, *Duck Tracks Returns* and *Blue Swan Songs* (and Blue Duck's sister label Blue Swan Records). Rusted Root, Brownie Mary, Psoas, Nixon Clocks and Out of the Blue were just some of the bands that had a relationship with the label and gained popularity in Pittsburgh playing at clubs like Graffiti, the Electric Banana, the Beehive and Nick's Fat City.

Freeman's connection to the alternative music scene in the city stretched to the previous decade. He had spent time at several different radio stations, including Slippery Rock University's student and faculty radio stations, before moving on to the University of Pittsburgh and serving as station manager at WPTS. He then served time at the nonprofit WYEP before being employed as a host of other stations, both in Pittsburgh and New York.

Perhaps most significant to the future Blue Duck Records was Freeman's founding of WXVS 1510-AM in Monroeville, an eastern suburb a little more than ten miles outside of Pittsburgh. X15, as it came to be known, was the city's first alternative station.

As Freeman recounted, the station was started with a punk DIY attitude closely related to much of the music and art created in the South Side that was centered on the Beehive a few short years later. "I had to start the AM station because I found it difficult to work someplace where other people had set things up and just be a cog in the machinery," he said. "I had done that at KISS 106.7, but I didn't like the commercialism. So, I avoided it."

After leaving X15, Freeman worked with Anthem Records and managed the Affordable Floors, considered by many to be Pittsburgh's most popular new wave dance band of the '80s. He also began teaching radio promotion at the Art Institute of Pittsburgh.

In 1992, Freeman decided to start Blue Duck Records as an opportunity to record and promote the music that interested him. His first release was with the post-punk band A.T.S. The band's music was well received by critics, and it brought attention to the new label. It was another band, however, that pushed the label to heights unimagined and forever tied Pittsburgh to a neo-hippie sound created by a music assemble that played acoustic guitars and African percussion.

Blue Duck's office space was initially located on Penn Avenue, next door to Rusted Root's practice space. The label released the band's CD *Cruel Sun* in 1993. Rusted Root gained first local and then national attention from the album and on the strength of their touring. They eventually moved to New York City and hired out-of-town management, and their careers took off when the band signed to Mercury Records and released *When I Woke*.

Freeman said that Rusted Root enabled him to check having a gold and, eventually, platinum album off his bucket list. The band also complicated things for Blue Duck Records. "It got my label on the map. Everyone knew who I was because of that, but everyone that came after that expected the same success as them," he said. "And that was really hard, because they were a one-in-several-blue-moons type of thing."

Both Liz Berlin and Jenn Wertz, members of Rusted Root, released tracks on the label's *Swan Songs*, portents of solo careers that would soon take flight.

Freeman came up with a clever marketing campaign while promoting the Blue Duck compilations. "I would make postcards with the bands and songs and send them with the CDs to radio stations, college radio stations, and we would ask them what songs they liked best, and they would send them back to us," he said. Blue Duck would then send the stations the full CDs of the artists selected. They would also send the recordings to music stores.

Freeman said that one of his biggest regrets was his inability to push Nixon Clocks to a larger audience. "They were the most meticulous musicians that I ever worked with. They were tight. You could see them at Nick's Fat City or in the studio, they sounded the same. They were professional. I loved working with them," he said.

Ultimately though, the label lost money on the band's release—not through any fault of their own. Rather, it spoke more to the changing music industry. "A lot of my product was with Camelot Music, and they went through a restructuring. They went through a hard time and went bankrupt. In the end, I had to take twenty cents to the dollar; it might have been less than that. I was devastated. It really hurt the label," he said.

After pushing so hard for rock and new wave artists, Freeman decided to focus on Blue Swan Records. "Blue Swan was me getting older. I liken it to deciding to have tea rather than a rum and coke," he said. "One thing that was nice about acoustic guitars was that you only had to have a small PA, one or two mics, and you could play anywhere."

Eventually, Freeman decided to close both Blue Duck and Blue Swan Records and go back to school.

The final release for the label was Lovechild's self-titled CD on Blue Swan Records.

Freeman has gone on to teach in Singapore but still recalls with fondness his time with Blue Duck Records. "This was probably the most awesome time in my life, without a doubt," he said. "I believe my heart was in the right place."

6

THE ARTISTS' LOFT

Wearing a motorcycle helmet on which he had painted a smiley face, Spaz was standing in the back of the Beehive reading the Dr. Seuss classic *Green Eggs and Ham* while hitting himself with a frying pan. The performance had started less confrontationally, but the drama had edged up as the local artist attempted to gain the focus of those in the café. "People weren't really paying attention," he remembered. "I was reading some poetry and trying to do a calm performance. People were there to just drink coffee and talk to their friends, so I went into the audience and bribed them with chocolate to pay attention. Then I just bashed myself over the head and screamed *Green Eggs and Ham*, and they loved it."

It was the artist's only performance at the South Side coffeehouse, but he said it was the Beehive's co-owner Scott Kramer who encouraged him to try something at the location.

Spaz said he initially had a conversation with Kramer and his partner, Steve Zumoff, about the idea of the coffeehouse as a place for people to perform and create art. "Scott told me to put something together for the Beehive. He said, 'Just show up, and you can do a performance.' He didn't ask me back," he said with a laugh.

The Greensburg native had a history of provocative performances. After leaving the eastern suburb for the more tolerant and experimental Pittsburgh, he performed with the all-drag punk band the Paul Lynde Experiment. He would also occasionally dress in drag and dance at various bands' performances. He said that most people in the city were receptive to

The schedule of shows at the South Side Beehive. *Scott Kramer and Steve Zumoff, private collection.*

his performances but remembered a time when the owner of one of the local clubs pulled him aside and cautioned him from dancing before a national act performed. "He was homophobic and possibly racist," Spaz remembered. "I was dressed like a cheerleader, and he was like, 'I want to warn you, they won't understand what you're doing here, and maybe you shouldn't dress in drag.' And I was thinking, 'You're just homophobic.'"

Spaz said, at that time, there were only small pockets of bohemian culture in the city, spotlighting both Chatham University's coffeehouse and the Beehive as examples. Perhaps that's why, when he thinks back to the early '90s and the art scene that was developing in Pittsburgh, he tends to remember it by the trope of one movie. "Whenever I think of that time, the late '80s and early '90s, I think of the movie *So I Married an Axe Murderer*, where he's doing really bad, clichéd beat poetry at a coffeehouse. That sums up that time for me," he said.

SPAZ'S BEEHIVE PERFORMANCE MIGHT have seemed out of place at other locales in the city. Certainly, it wouldn't have found a home in neighborhoods like Shadyside, which had started as a hippie hangout but had morphed into a high-priced yuppie destination. The Beehive, however, with its brightly colored, hand-painted walls, secondhand furniture and grunge-inspired fashions, was the right place at the right time for both Spaz and others who were experimenting with all genres of art.

In fact, it might have become a bad stereotype, but the Beehive tended to offer a safe place for the type of Gen X, heavy-handed, shoe-gazing art, music and poetry that was a hallmark of the '90s. It was also a safe place for those who were struggling against this scene, creating works that were, at times, confrontational and, at other times, just plain odd. Anyone trying to create, it seemed, was welcome at the coffeehouse.

DAMON GRIFFITH GREW UP in Beechview, a city neighborhood bordering the South Hills suburbs of Dormont and Green Tree. He was, by his own admission, "a little weird." He remembers that people would sometimes cross the street first to harass him in high school and then, eventually, to avoid him. "We stopped being weird little geeky kids and became these weirdos—they did not understand," he remembered.

Damon found a home at the Beehive.

Like so many others, he was a patron of the coffeehouse, an employee and an artist who drew inspiration from its community and used it as a springboard for his artistic endeavors. "There was the whole Gen X freak thing happening on the South Side, where I didn't feel threatened or judged. This was our turf," he said. "We were comfortable." The Beehive was filled with "a bunch of freaks wanting to do poetry and music," Damon recalled. It was that desire that led him to create the Bull Seal Collective, an artistic troupe based around his poetry and music that included, among others, Phat Man Dee.

The idea for the collective came out of Damon's frustration with an aborted music career in which he felt he was unable to find an identity. The musician/writer said he had kept a notebook in his pocket in which he wrote down odd thoughts as they occurred.

While accompanying local writer/musician/artist Bob Ziller to a poetry reading in West Virginia, Damon decided to storm the stage and read some of the poems he had been writing in his pocket notebook. The pieces, he said, were nonsense, but in many ways, they were written as a reaction against much of the self-indulgent work he saw other Gen Xers creating. It was, in fact, the very thing Spaz was reacting against in his art. Griffith would eventually add music and, realizing it would be helpful to have others who shared his outlook as partners, brought in Phat Man Dee. "She understood it and got it, whereas other people understood it but didn't get it, and some got it but didn't understand it," he said.

The collective, he explained, was meant to be a revolving door that people would come in and out. Unfortunately, Damon never found all of the right people at the right time to fulfill his vision.

One of the most popular happenings created by the Bull Seal Collective was the annual Ides of March March, something he said that was created to mess with what he called the "tourists," or those who came to the South Side mainly on the weekend to drink with no regard for the neighborhood's culture. Damon's wife, Sabrina, said the march was started as a reaction to the frat boy crowd who populated East Carson Street on Friday and Saturday nights, making the women who lived in and around the neighborhood feel unsafe.

And while the Ides of March March didn't happen in the Beehive, Damon said that it happened because the Beehive was there, providing a safe spot for the artists and those who felt different. "It was the catalyst for us all

While the line between employee and customer was often fluid, there were some places meant only for those who worked at the coffeehouse. *Scott Kramer and Steve Zumoff, private collection.*

A self-portrait by a former Beehive employee who eventually died by suicide. *Scott Kramer and Steve Zumoff, private collection.*

to be in that neighborhood and for those things to happen, because we were all together," he explained.

Even after Damon and Sabrina left Pittsburgh, the Ides of March March continued to exist. In 2023, Phat Man Dee persisted with the tradition, moving the event to Allentown—another Pittsburgh neighborhood that hasn't recovered from the collapse of the steel mills but has begun to show signs of artistic seeds and even features its own independent café, Black Forge Coffee.

AND WHILE THE BEEHIVE didn't invent the underground art scene in the city, it did give those artists who lived and congregated on the South Sides a place to meet, discuss their work and plan collaborations. It also served as a base for those who did not work in a visual medium. In fact, some of the painters and sculptors who would soon make the Beehive their home had already been working, living and meeting in the neighborhood.

Scott Kramer remembered the Baba Club, which served as a part retail space, part artist hangout. The owner said he would go to the various thrift shops located near the neighborhood to buy jeans, which he would then paint and resell. "There were a bunch of artists and students from the Art Institute of Pittsburgh that hung out there. They were able to live in the South Side because the rent was cheap. It closed right before we opened, and a lot of the artists migrated to the Beehive," he said.

Another space that was important to the scene began as a brewery, making beer as part of the Duquesne Brewing Company. According to the Brew House Artists Loft's website, the brewery had been open for seventy-three years before competition forced its closure in 1972. After remaining dormant for over a decade, the building found new life as a study and eventually residential space for local artists. In the '90s, around the same time the Beehive opened, the artists relocated there and started organizing. And in 1993, the space officially became the Brew House Association.

Rich Bach had a studio at the Brew House until 2015, when he said more "civilians" began overtaking the building. So, too, did Beehive regular Lloyd Wilson. "I rented the seventh and eighth floors for $125 a month, and they paid gas and electric," he remembered.

Lloyd Wilson, a seventy-eight-year-old sculptor and painter, worked as a night watchman at Chatham Village on Mount Washington, which allowed him to pay the rent on his studio and maintain his standing as an amateur

Lloyd Wilson talks with Judy Dickson and an unknown person. *Photograph provided by Scott Kramer and Steve Zumoff.*

artist—this, despite having his work on display as part of the Carnegie Museum of Art's permanent collection. Theo Logos recalled Wilson as debonair and as someone who always had a group of interesting people around him. The artist, he said, was one of the keys to the South Side art scene. "He was an example of someone who had lived life on his own terms, and he seemed to be doing OK," Logos said.

As part of the Pittsburgh art scene from the '70s, Lloyd was involved with many of the different organizations that helped support artists and their work, including the Associated Artists of Pittsburgh, which was founded in 1910. He said that he discovered the Beehive, which provided a third space for him away from work and the studio, during a walk through the neighborhood. "I loved it. If I wasn't working on a project, I knew where I was going. I was going to the Beehive, because there was always someone who agreed with you and someone to argue with," he said. "That's the thing about the Beehive. We had poets, people who wrote music…very, very talented people."

And unlike present-day coffeehouses, the café provided an opportunity for cross-pollination with other artists, Wilson said, noting that, today, most people in places like Starbucks tend to have their faces focused on their computers or phones and are unwilling to talk to others sitting near them—the antithesis of what took place at the Beehive.

TIM KAULEN REMEMBERED SCOTT from the time the Beehive owner knocked on the door of the recording studio where he worked, catty-corner to the new coffeehouse, and introduced himself. The drugstore had long lingered in the artist's mind. "Not to be disparaging, but it was freaky," he said. "You could go in there and tell the man you weren't feeling well and what you were feeling, and he would make you a concoction of medicine without a prescription. It was bizarre."

Tim moved to Pittsburgh from Mercer County in 1984 to attend the Art Institute. He lived in a dorm at Duquesne University and would walk across the Tenth Street Bridge, a bridge that would soon become meaningful in Tim's life, to the South Side, where he would buy beer.

Tim said that in the mid-'80s, the South Side still housed a generation of people who had grown up in the shadow of the steel industry. "The population tabled. The seniors were still there, which allowed for a cohesive community with real culture and real tradition," he said. "It was wonderful to be a young person there."

Community wasn't the only thing Kaulen found on the South Side. "There was a lot of opportunity for space, because like most Mon Valley mill towns, there was this period of decline from 1975 to 1990," he said. But as he soon found out, the area offered plenty of unused and abandoned warehouses and storefronts, perfect for an artist just starting out.

After spending time working at an audio-visual studio, Tim was laid off and began receiving unemployment benefits. He viewed this as a chance to do nothing but create art—he simply needed to find a space.

An abandoned building near the Tenth Street Bridge seemed perfect for what he had in mind. "I barricaded myself in the building for a year," he said. "I had these two floors and decorated them. I collected trash and furniture to create painting and artwork out of." The building, he noted, was next to a mill on one side—long gone—and an empty office building on the other.

"I had an ongoing feud with a homeless encampment in the office building. I would collect furniture from the trash and make this artwork in all kinds of weird shapes. When I would go out, the homeless people would come in and take the furniture," he said. Tim first tried to reason with the people, making signs asking them not to steal the furniture. When that didn't work, he began breaking a leg off of each piece he brought in, rendering it worthless for its original intent.

He also had to contend with high school students who learned about where he was squatting and what he was doing. They took it as a challenge to break into the building and destroy everything he created.

The changing landscape presented prospects as well. Abandoned mills, decaying bridges and deserted industrial sites were fraught with the opportunity to be scavenged and create art on their grounds. "The destruction of the J and L steel mill was probably one of the biggest factors of my life. That allowed me to seize the opportunity of change and transition and growth," he said.

By the early '90s, Tim was working at the Brew House, and he became friends with the other artists there. The group made Sunday rituals of exploring the shuttered steel mills. They salvaged what they could but also created art in some of the industrial sites they explored along the Monongahela and Allegheny Rivers. "It was through seeing all of the vacancy and emptiness that we started building stuff in those places. At first, we would go in and scavenge and stack stuff and tie it together and take pictures and leave it, but with a little cohesion of thoughts and ideas, we began to make stuff in abandoned buildings in different vacant buildings. The South Side became hosts to that in different venues and buildings," he said.

Tim's best-known work was a piece of unsanctioned public art on the Tenth Street Bridge.

In the late '80s, Tim painted four geese, sometimes mistaken for dinosaurs, on the south tower of the bridge in memory of his late grandfather. The geese were briefly removed in 2017, when the bridge was repainted after a rehabilitation project. Tim started a petition, and after nearly one thousand people signed in support of returning the geese, city council voted and agreed to let the artist repaint the icons—at his own cost.

Tim said that after spending time with Scott and Steve, there was an immediate connection, something that carried forward when he made some of the sculptures that were at both the Beehive and Lava Lounge, a bar the two bought on the South Side after the success of the café. The location of the bar had a storied history in the neighborhood. It was formerly called the Liberty Bell and was home to local legend Frank Capri, a quirky Pittsburgh performer known as much for his pompadour as he was for his shows.

It was after Bob Ziller opened his gallery, Tim said, that many of the artists found a place to exhibit in the neighborhood.

ACCORDING TO MANY, ZILLER was the hub of the art scene that was developing at the Beehive and around the city's South Side neighborhood.

A Pittsburgh transplant, Ziller hitchhiked to Pittsburgh in 1991 from New Jersey. He was following a friend who had already left the East Coast for Los Angeles to start a vague musical project, but he said it was more of a whim than any concrete plan.

With a résumé similar to that of City Lights Bookstore owner/publisher and Beat writer Lawrence Ferlinghetti, Bob wore many hats: musician, artist, publisher, translator, poet and gallery owner, to name a few. He served the same function as Ferlinghetti: making connections, trading ideas, forging relationships and pushing the neighborhoods he lived in the same way the West Coast poet did for San Francisco beginning in the 1950s.

Bob met his contacts in the Pittsburgh art world while he was working at the Beehive. He also lived, with several other South Side artists, at Hellrose Place, although Theo Logos was quick to point out that while others reveled in the squalor that was part of the bohemian lifestyle, Bob's apartment was always immaculate.

The future gallerist said that the Beehive was one of the first places he found in Pittsburgh. He said he arrived in Pittsburgh on a rainy day, and the café was the first interesting place he came upon. It would soon become

Right: Bob Ziller. *Photograph by David Grim.*

Opposite: A sign advertising artwork that was for sale at the Beehive. *Scott Kramer and Steve Zumoff, private collection.*

his main stop. "I would go there because I could just order a pot of tea and hang out," he said. "I got hired at the time they had bought the building in Oakland. I ended up painting the ceiling of the theater—it was all just eyes." Once his painting was complete, Ziller saw the opportunity for more work and stayed on, assisting with the construction of the Beehive's second location. When the coffeehouse opened, Bob became a janitor before taking on the same role on the South Side.

The neighborhood, he remembered, was composed mostly of shot-and-beer bars, small galleries and a string of bookstores, including City Books, Riverrun Books, Eljay Books and St. Elmo's Books and Music. Bob even opened his own bookstore years later in the revitalized downtown. Awesome Books was a pop-up bookstore in the city's new Cultural District that was home to most of its theaters, cabaret clubs and art galleries in what was once the region's red-light district.

The South Side, he said, felt alive and blooming with inspiration at the time. "There was a lot of creativity there, and it was filled with artists and cheap places to live. I think I was paying $200 a month. Then I moved up the hill and was paying $300 for a month for a whole house. I had a lot of friends that bought houses for like $6,000 or $10,000 or $18,000 back before the *New York Times* wrote an article about what a great area it was. Then the gentrification happened," he said.

During his time at the coffeehouse, Bob opened Lascaux Gallery, first out of his home in Mount Washington and then moving it to East Carson Street when he relocated to the South Side. Café owner Scott Kramer began to

visit the gallery and saw that Bob had an aptitude for hanging art. He asked if he would consider curating shows at the Beehive as well.

Bob said Kramer and Zumoff had a fairly liberal approach to what got hung at the coffeehouse: if someone had enough work, it was presented. Mostly, he said, people simply came and asked if they could have their work shown, and he said yes.

In addition to the gallery and bookstore, Bob started a small publishing house, Lascaux Editions, which published two books of translations, his own poetry and several works by other authors. In his own collection, *Van Gogh Sitting,* Ziller included a few poems inspired by or about the Beehive and its various regulars. In "Early Birds," he wrote:

Opening the coffeehouse again,
here I am, the janitor serving coffee and tea,
burning bagels and botching cappuccinos.

It happens time after time,
whenever one of the young morning girls
gets a new boyfriend,
you just can't drag her out of bed.

He also found inspiration writing about Phat Man Dee, East Carson Street and another artist who was a regular at the Beehive: Bill Patterson. So moved was Bob by his sketches that he produced the book *Pit Stops for Angels,* a collection of the artist's work.

PATTERSON WAS TYPICAL OF many who called the South Side home in the early '90s. Older than the art students who would soon become the neighborhood's regulars, he had previously worked as a steel worker. Despite having a lifestyle that seemed ill fit for success, he appeared to have worked his way into the heart of Beehive regulars and employees. A prodigious drinker, according to many, he spent much of his day inside the coffeehouse with a pad, sketching the regulars, various bands and musicians and scenes around the South Side of the city. When he wasn't at the coffeehouse, Bill

A Bill Patterson drawing. *Scott Kramer and Steve Zumoff, private collection.*

could be found at Dee's, a shot-and-beer bar that would soon change its look and become a second home many at the Beehive. In fact, several of the Beehive's workers thought of it as a sister shop that served alcohol. Not only would they while away their non-working hours there, but they would also spend holidays with the bar's employees.

Bill had fallen in love with art as a child, taking lessons at the Carnegie Museum of Art. When he retired in 1986, after thirty-five years of labor in the steel mills—and, at times, at a second job—he devoted himself full time to drawing. He also attended the Great Peach March for Nuclear Disarmament, walking from Los Angeles to Washington, D.C.*

In Bob's book of Patterson's work, John Bender said, "Bill is the glue that holds all of Pittsburgh together." Indeed, it seems he made his mark on the South Side before his death.

Lloyd Wilson remembers Patterson as someone who was often seen on the South Side riding a bicycle with a basket on the front.

Natalie Gilchrist said that Patterson taught her how to reuse mailers that included postage on them as a way to send letters for free, something Beehive

---

* Taken from *Pit Stop for the Angels: Sketches by Bill Patterson* (Pittsburgh, PA: Lascaux Editions, 1993).

employee Leslie Donovan recalled the artist doing as well. In fact, Patterson would often pen letters to Donovan while she stood in front of him. So deep were her memories that Donovan began tearing up nearly thirty years later while recalling that Bob Ziller, who took possession of Patterson's bike after he died, let her ride it. "I took it all the way down to the Terminal Building. I looked around and was crying my eyes out the entire time, I assure you," she said. "But Bob knew it would make me feel better."

Before Vincent Musi and his wife, Callie Shell, were married; before they were renowned photographers with bylines in *National Geographic*, *People* and *Life*; before she worked for CNN; before she was Al Gore's official photographer; before he published the book *The Year of the Dog*; and before the two started a popular Instagram account focused on dogs, they were Pittsburgh photographers furloughed from their roles at the *Pittsburgh Press*.

The *Press* was a daily newspaper that had been in existence since 1884. At one time, it was the second-largest newspaper in the state, its circulation only behind the *Philadelphia Inquirer*'s. In 1992, a teamster strike stopped publication of the Pittsburgh paper, and while the labor dispute was negotiated, employees were forced to sit idle waiting for the strike to

Vice President Al Gore drinks from a Beehive mug. *Photograph by Callie Shell.*

end. That never happened, however, and the *Press* was bought by another Pittsburgh newspaper, the *Pittsburgh Gazette*. The merger created the *Pittsburgh Post-Gazette*.

"There was a time when we were sold off like office furniture," Vince remembered. "They paid us essentially not to work. We didn't have anything to do, anything to put out." Callie said that, despite being on strike, in order to be paid, they had to come into the office every day, which they dutifully did. "We would spend half our day there and half our day going to this bar nearby or going to the Beehive and having coffee," she said.

Vince said that a colleague of the couple and member of the Silver Eye Center for Photography, Bill Wade, suggested the pair try the coffeehouse, which had just opened. It was so new that Scott's "Artists Wanted" was still hanging in the window. "It grew out of nothing pretty quickly," he said. "We felt like we discovered something. Here it was. The streets were still kind of quiet. A lot of the businesses were still closed. It was a beacon."

The murals were what caught Vince's eye the first time he stepped into the café, as they made him feel as if he were on another planet.

Callie said that the pair, slightly older than many of the shop's original patrons, were pioneers in a sense and were seen by some in the community as fact finders. "There was a gyro place across the street, and I went in there to pick up a sandwich. They were like, 'We just saw you come out of that place. We've heard rumors that they sell coffee for more than a dollar.' Another time, I went in and asked if they'd been over for a coffee, and they said yes and that it was really helping to have so much more foot traffic." Callie found that to be true. When she was at the Beehive, she was more likely to stop at a restaurant or store nearby.

The coffeehouse also played a vital role in the budding relationship between Callie and Vince. The pair had just started dating and used the coffeehouse as a safe place to meet since they weren't supposed to date people from the paper, she remembered.

While they were not part of the South Side's scene of artists and musicians, the two soon made friends with the owners, who were closer to their age than many who frequented the coffeehouse. She said that Scott, especially, acted as a sort of ambassador, introducing them to other people. "He knew everyone," Callie said, "and kept up on where they worked. He really endeavored to endear them to the place around them that had been there a long time."

The four became such good friends that Scott and Steve attended the wedding of Vince and Callie. Of course, they found a way to make their

Customers sit in front of the Beehive's mural featuring a coffee cup like the one painted by Pittsburgh artist Burton Morris. *Photograph provided by Scott Kramer and Steve Zumoff.*

time pay off. "We had a bluegrass band, and the next morning, when we went to clean up, there were Scott and Steve to carry all the kegs with the leftover beer," Callie said with a laugh.

Vince feels that the time in which the Beehive opened lent itself to creating relationships that lasted. "There was no internet, we didn't have cellphones and, of course, the tables were on top of one another. So, how could you not be expected to meet people?" he said.

The relationship between the pair and the coffeehouse helped create a unique opportunity for the Beehive: a photograph of then–vice president Al Gore drinking from a mug with the café's logo.

The couple had moved from Pittsburgh to South Carolina when Callie was offered the opportunity to photograph Barack Obama. Her photographs became both a *Time* magazine story documenting the president's first one hundred days in office and a more personal book, *Hope, Never Fear: A Personal Portrait of the Obamas.*

She was then offered the opportunity to serve as the former president's official photographer but turned it down out of concern for her family life and her ability to serve as a mother. She did, however, accept the same role with Al Gore after being told she could define the parameters of the job.

Original artwork of the Beehive bought at auction by the owners. *Scott Kramer and Steve Zumoff, private collection.*

Callie and Vince moved to Washington, D.C., for the new position. "We went from shooting pool and drinking coffee to working in the office by 7:00 a.m.," she said.

The relocation, Callie explained, was like moving away to college. And like college freshmen, when they returned home for a visit, they noted that the South Side had evolved a little more from its blue-collar roots. "Each time back, it was like there's another new place that opened and another new place that opened," she said.

It was because of her relationship with the vice president that she was able to capture a picture of Gore holding a mug with the coffeehouse's logo. "He was doing a speech in Pittsburgh and said he was going to go to the 'O' in Oakland, and I said, 'You've got to go to the Beehive. It was responsible for the whole rebirth of the South Side,'" she said. "And so, he got a picture with the mug instead because he was curious. He said something like, 'I'm told I'm really missing out on something.'"

ARTISTS OF ALL MEDIUMS found like-minded creatives at the café. They were also given the opportunity to experiment and find their voice there.

Photographer David Grim first started going to the Beehive in 1992 during his first year of graduate school before he began working as a coffee slinger at the Oakland location. "I was always interested in stuff that wasn't mainstream," he said. "That's what drove me there." David said his employment at the Beehive allowed him to meet other creatives who both worked at and frequented the coffeehouse, including TV On the Radio's Kyp Malone and Aaron Aites, a local filmmaker who made a documentary about the death metal scene in Europe before passing away.

David said that he, too, harbored dreams of working in film but settled on photography due to the cost of equipment. "I wanted to make movies, but when I bought my equipment in 2001, I couldn't really afford a digital video camera, so I thought, 'OK, I'll get a camera and learn to do photography for a couple of years until digital equipment gets cheaper,'" he explained. David began taking the camera with him as he went about his day, and soon, people identified him as a photographer.

The Sharpsburg resident said that he had two shows at the Beehive. The first was a mishmash of photographs he had collected from carrying the camera with him and learning how to use it. The show featured a lot of weird roadside attractions, he said. The second was more provocative. "Somewhere outside of Morgantown, someone had built a Bible walk in the '60s or '70s out of old store mannequins. They had these outdoor shelters for each vignette. It was created by the Jesuits or another brotherhood in the woods, but the monastery had closed," he remembered. David went on a trip to document the scenes with Beehive co-owner Scott Kramer. "It was pretty degraded, but I got these cool shots of the Last Supper and one of Scott where he has his legs up on Jesus. It was so great."

ERICA DILCER WAS INTRODUCED to the Beehive through her friend and co-owner Steve Zimmer. She remembered going to the coffeehouse with her now ex-husband and former Kelly Affair lead singer, John Bechdel.

She morphed into a photographer during her time with Bechdel at the Beehive. "It was 1991. I bought a camera right before Earth Day. I remember because I went out shooting for the day, and that was my first real experience," she said.

Erica started taking photographs of her boyfriend and his band, along with other musicians around town when they played shows.

Like it did for so many other artists at the time, the South Side and its developing art scene allowed Erica to experiment and learn her craft while supporting other artists. She said she used to keep a notebook of exposures and settings she used and would often refer back to it as she photographed various bands in different clubs and bars.

But it was while Erica was working at Bernie's Photo Center, a Pittsburgh mainstay on East Ohio Street on the city's North Side, that she found her first break. "Somebody from one of the papers called and said the Chili Peppers were in town and their photographer hadn't shown up. They asked if we knew anyone. I said yes, took a camera, went to lunch and I went and shot the band," she said.

Erica eventually got a gig working for Sony Music, shooting bands during their meet and greets with fans. Her style—professional and unobtrusive—eventually landed her at the top of the call list when bands, music papers and publications needed photographs.

The photographer wasn't just involved in her own projects. She worked to help Bechdel promote the band and even created the paint the singer coated himself in before performances.

"The South Side is this island of misfit toys. The people who have never left these few blocks in their life have a flavor about them. I feel like they created a friendly, nonjudgmental, artsy place because they didn't have anywhere to go, and it's expanded into other buildings," she said.

JOSH SPENCE IDENTIFIED THE Beehive as a magical place the moment he walked in the door.

Josh was a student at the Art Institute of Pittsburgh who grew up in Huntington, West Virginia. "I was a country boy. I had never been anywhere," he said. "I had culture shock for the first six months I was here."

Josh found an apartment in Lawrenceville, which was still suffering through the worst of its postindustrial morass. He discovered the Beehive shortly after moving to the city. "I don't have memory of the first time I entered the Beehive, other than it was magical," he said. "I went back every day. I lived there until I graduated." The photography student said the coffeehouse became a home away from home—so much so that Scott hired him, first at the Lava Lounge and later as a coffee slinger at the Beehive.

In addition to photography, Josh plays bass. It's a relationship that has paid dividends in his professional life, as his art has appeared on several bands' CD covers, as well as on posters promoting their shows.

Wild Raspberry Hot Chocolate
Medium Hot Chocolate with a shot of raspberry syrup, topped with whipped cream. ~ $2.10

Hot Vanilla Cream
Medium mug of Steamed Milk with a shot of vanilla syrup. ~ $1.80

Vanilla Latte
Medium Latte with a shot of vanilla. Very popular ~ $2.75

Hot Apple Cider
(when available) Fresh from the farm 16 ounce glass ~ $1.75

Atomic Buzzer
Large House Coffee with Two Shots of Espresso ~ $2.00

Choco Buzzer
Large House Coffee with two shots of Espresso and a smooth shot of Chocolate ~ $2.15

Beehive Coffeehouses
3807 Forbes, Oakland and
1327 E. Carson st., Southside

Flavored hot drink menu. *Scott Kramer and Steve Zumoff, private collection.*

He's also served as a studio consultant, booked musical acts at various locations and worked for the Northeast Kentucky Arts Council and at several different art galleries.

He's been out of the art scene for a while but has moved back to Pittsburgh and restarted his career. He said that he's leaning on relationships he built during his time at the Beehive and is hoping to work with other alums from the coffeehouse. And if his art career doesn't pick up again, Josh has another plan: "Owning a coffeehouse has always been a long-term goal," he said.

IT WAS MORE THAN visual and conceptual artists who stopped in for an espresso at the Beehive. Black Sheep Puppet Festival, a South Side mainstay at the Brew House, was started by a group of creatives that included Rob Long.

The festival, at one time the oldest puppet festival in the country, brought together performers and volunteers from across the United States.

Before his time at Brew House, however, Rob discovered the Beehive with a girlfriend who was a year older than he was. The pair used to walk to the South Side and found the coffeehouse among the art scene that was growing in the neighborhood. "It was pretty cool," he said. "It showed me what living in the city could mean."

Rob said that in the early years of the festival, a synergy existed between the Beehive and the artists. The café would bring coffee to the puppeteers, and the puppeteers, in their downtime, would visit the coffeehouse.

"There was this period where the South Side was weird and it was artistic," he remembered. "It was very fringe. At the time, Pittsburgh was very isolated. People from the South Side didn't venture to other territories—neither did students at CMU or Pitt or people from Squirrel Hill. That mixing started to happen, and part of that is because of Scott and Steve."

Long had studied theater, lighting design and architecture at Carnegie Mellon University, but like so many other artists at the time, he didn't finish his training there. Instead, he taught himself photography and spent a little over a decade concentrating on that. Eventually, his work, which centered on Beehive customers and South Side regulars, would appear in most of the city's publications. He would branch out to architectural photography before shifting gears again.

Rob eventually started Clear Story Studio, a team of professional artists, designers and technicians who work to create visual and spatial experiences that communicate new narrative forms. A small sampling of what Clear Story has done includes the lighting for a recent Andy Warhol exhibit focused on the Velvet Underground; lighting and theatrical systems at the August Wilson House; lighting renovations at Highmark Fifth Avenue Place; and fabrication and other work with artist Florentijn Hofman's *Rubber Duck*, which became a sensation in the city during its time afloat in the Three Rivers, as well as many other projects. All of these, Rob explained, allow

A hand-drawn Beehive advertisement rarely seen in the age of desktop publishing. *Scott Kramer and Steve Zumoff, private collection.*

him to operate behind the scenes with an invisible hand and make things happen by producing images, experiences, lighting designs and more. "We help create spaces for people to inhabit and get a feeling without necessarily knowing that I had anything to do with it," he said.

Jason Kirin started his artistic life as a kid from Monroeville, Pennsylvania, who wore all black and dyed his hair the same color. He said he didn't set out to be a goth; instead, he was simply colorblind but quickly fell into the lifestyle. "I got mistaken for a goth kid by this other goth kid named Ben. We started to become really close friends. And it was just like a comedy, because it was just my black clothes, but he was like, 'Oh, there's somebody that's similar to me," he remembered.

Jason's friend had an apartment behind Club Laga on East Carson Street, and it wasn't long before the two ended up at the Beehive. The coffeehouse, Jason said, proved to be a gathering place for him and his friends after their poetry readings in the glass court between the Carnegie Library and the parking lot on the corner of Murray and Forbes Avenues in Squirrel Hill were moved there. "That was great," he said, "because we would leave at midnight and go back to Ben's apartment with all these drunk poets and read until the sun came up."

Not only did the Beehive provide a performance space for Jason, but it also gave him a space to work. "I would sit there and smoke my Lucky Strikes and write in my moleskin notebook," he said.

Like many who weren't part of the core group of artists and South Side denizens who frequented the Beehive, Jason said he often experienced imposter syndrome at the café. "There was no reason for that, but I remember that everyone was so creative and making the most incredible art I had ever seen, and I was like, 'Please don't look at me, please don't look at me.' I just thought everyone there was so much cooler than me."

For many, games like *Magic: The Gathering* were way to fill time at the Beehive. For Rhonda Libbey, fantasy artwork became a vocation.

Rhonda said that she started coming to the Beehive in the mid-'90s, when she was a student at the Art Institute of Pittsburgh. Her friend had found the coffeehouse while on a date and told her about it. "I was like, 'That sounds like a lovely place.' We loved coffeehouses and diners," she said. "It was so arty and had a friendly environment and was cool and fun."

After graduation, Rhonda found herself in the unusual job of painting ornamental flatware for the interior design store Pelora before she began doing design and prepress work. She wanted, however, to be an illustrator and work with games like *Dungeons and Dragons*.

Her work now appears in classics like *Call of Cthulhu*, as well as the Beehive favorite *Magic*.

Rhonda's husband is also involved in the arts, working as a professional photographer and making art reproductions.

The Beehive, Rhonda said, could be either an incubator for work or a more relaxed experience. "You can have a lot of really interesting conversations with people, or you could kick back and work on something or maybe make a new friend," she said.

Like many others, Rhonda said her South Side circle grew beyond the coffeehouse, eventually including Dee's, the Eye of Horus and Slacker. But the Beehive, she said, is responsible for some of the most colorful relationships in her life, including those with Phat Man Dee and members of the Bull Seal Collective. "When I think of the South Side, I think of that community and all of those connections, and it still gives me the warm fuzzies," she said. "I know it's not that anymore, but that's the way I continue to see it."

NOT ALL THE ARTISTS who came out of the Beehive were involved in highbrow activities like painting or photography. Some gravitated toward different types of performance art. Eric Simon, also known as Skippy, is an example of such an artist.

Now living in California and involved in stand-up comedy, among other pursuits, Skippy was originally a disaffected youth, typical of many Gen Xers. By his own account, Skippy wasn't a great student, drifting in and out of trouble. "I was part of an antiracist skinhead movement and belonged to a gang called the Potato Skins. We were straight-edge and sharp—Skinheads Against Racial Prejudice."

He signed up for a tour of duty with the military while he was still in high school. When he returned to the city, he started going to the South Side Beehive to play pinball. His goals at the time, he said, were pretty basic. "I wanted to hang out at the Beehive, play pinball and do a bunch of acid. I just became a regular."

Skippy started working at the Oakland location, first as a coffee slinger and later as a manager of the store.

Beehive Coffeehouse & Dessertery
1327 E. Carson Street
Pittsburgh, PA 15203
Ph. (412) 488-HIVE
Fx. (412) 481-7445

Mr. Robert Rifkin
Schapira't Coffee & Tea Co.
P.O. Box 327 - Factory Lane
Pine Plains, New York 12567

Dear Mr. Rifkin,

The Beehive has experienced a warm welcome into the Pittsburgh business community. In response to the excitement created by our original establishment, we have decided to expand with the opening of a coffeehouse/theater. This new Beehive is located in the heart of the University of Pittsburgh and is easily accessible from two other universities and colleges. Providing that this second location is also successful, future expansion plans include a location in the downtown business center and a location in the Squirell Hill area.

We are planning to increase the awareness of the city to the fine coffees available, the history of coffee, our different types of preparation, and the available means for these preparations. In order to accomplish this we are planning on printing a series of brochure covering the forementioned topics. Artists and writers are currently working on this project. We are also planning on having bags printed which will feature a special logo designed for the Beehive.

Currently there are four different brochures which have a printing cost of $2,500 for 10,000 of each type. The cost of the bags is $.20 each with a minimum order of 30,000. The printing costs for this plan come to $16,000 which does not include the associated art costs. We have a strong resolve towards the expansion of our business to coincide with the promotion of our products that feature the excellent quality of Shapira's coffee. However, a problem arises with the additional costs that this printing will cost. Currently there is in excess of $140,000 invested in the opening of our second Beehive. We are asking Shapira's assistance in the financing of the printing costs in the following fashion, an equal split of the $16,000 plus a low interest loan to cover the Beehive's $8,000. We hope that you will share our enthusiasm for our expansion to generate mutual benefits. Thank you for your time and consideration in this matter.

Respectfully yours,

Scott Kramer   Steven Zumoff

A note written to the Beehive's coffee suppliers after a second location was opened. Interestingly, Scott and Steve mention future expansion plans that never materialized. *Scott Kramer and Steve Zumoff, private collection.*

He remembered that each August, as college students would begin moving into the neighborhood to attend one of the local universities, there was an influx of what the employees affectionately called "freakies." "The clientele was mostly college kids, ravers and people that wanted to play *Magic: The Gathering* and hippies having an identity crisis," he noted.

His time at the Beehive belied his true ambition: to be a stand-up comedian. "When I was sixteen, my parents would take [me] to the Funny Bone at Station Square, and I would do stand-up. I sucked, but I did it," he said. "When I got out of the military, I tried it again." After moving to California, Skippy continued to try his hand at the craft. He performed at the Comedy Store.

But was the internet and a meta video that caused Skippy and one of his videos to go viral.

A decade ago, the comedian performed a skit at a club in Pasadena, where he imitated Black people reacting to comedy routines. The video became a hit as others made videos of Black people reacting to his original routine. "It's pretty stupid, but what can I say?" he commented.

As A GENERATION OF artists and musicians began thinking of the South Side Beehive as a home away from home, Scott and Steve started to think of expanding the café's reach. For that, they looked east.

A postcard sold at the Beehive. *Scott Kramer and Steve Zumoff, private collection.*

7

THE SOUTH SIDE BEEHIVE BURNS IN HELL

Scott Kramer said that as he looked down East Carson Street and saw people waiting in line to get into the Beehive the day it opened, he had one thought: "We should open up another one of these."

And in 1992, that's what Scott and his partner, Steve Zumoff, did.

The pair decided that for their second go 'round, they would open a coffeehouse in the neighborhood they had originally considered and one they were already familiar with: Oakland. Scott grew up in the city's East End, and both men had attended college at the University of Pittsburgh in the heart of the neighborhood.

A real estate company suggested a building known as Kings Court Theater on Forbes Avenue. The space had originally served as a jail—and then as a police station, firehouse and retail store—before George and Ernest Stern of Associated Theatres occupied the building in 1965 and turned it into a first-run movie theater. In 1976, the theater screened its first midnight feature of *The Rocky Horror Picture Show*. The film would return on a semiregular basis throughout the early '80s. The cult classic played steadily beginning in 1988 until the theater closed in 1990.

The new location was huge—six thousand square feet compared to the one thousand square feet at the South Side location. It included two rooms upstairs, the movie theater and a space downstairs that served coffee and desserts. "The idea was that if you open a place six times as large, you'll make six times as much money," Scott said. "Turns out, it doesn't work that way."

Above: A note faxed from the Oakland location to the South Side Beehive. *Scott Kramer and Steve Zumoff, private collection.*

Left: A newspaper article discussing the transformation from King's Court to the Beehive. *Scott Kramer and Steve Zumoff, private collection.*

Since the building was located close to several hospitals, Scott and Steve believed the nurses and doctors would prove to be faithful clientele of the coffeehouse. That never happened. "It turned out that after working on their feet for twelve hours, they opted to go home," Scott said.

The café was able to pull patrons from the colleges and universities located near the store, including the University of Pittsburgh, Carnegie Mellon University, Carlow College and Pittsburgh Filmmakers, in addition to some of the nearby secondary schools, along with students from Oakland Catholic and Taylor Allderdice High School, which future South Side Beehive mainstay Phat Man Dee attended. The future South Side janitor and Pittsburgh performer said she used to go to the Oakland coffeehouse to do her homework or meet her friends. "We would see concerts, hear music and poetry readings—all the 'things,'" she said. "Before cellphones and pagers, if you wanted to find your people and figure out what you were doing, that's where you went."

The Kings Court location needed its interior to be updated before the Beehive could open, but this time, the previous scheme of trading work and art for tokens was more challenging. Artists flocked to the East Carson Street location, happy to paint and decorate the store—not so this time. "I'll call the design—Oakland versus South Side—a struggle. It was significantly bigger, and the artists were a little less excited. Instead of doing a small area, they were doing bigger areas, and I think the token deal was a little less successful. But people were interested nonetheless," Scott noted.

South Side Beehive stalwart Bob Ziller was part of the team that worked at the new location. He painted a series of eyes that looked down on the patrons. Once he was finished with his task, he remained part of the construction crew that was rehabilitating the theater.

Scott said that some of the furniture purchased for the second location came from another Pittsburgh landmark: the Syria Mosque. "They were closing down. They had this big sale. We went and bought a bunch of stuff to decorate the building: chairs, a cool couch, this cool metal grid," he said. Steve said that some of the items were rather odd, and some people assumed they were leftover from the building's time as a jail. "There was a cage and this big glass jug," he said. "It had this fake blood in it. It was bizarre and probably something they used for Halloween."

Local artist Mike Saxman did much of the design for the bar on the second floor of the coffeehouse that was added after a few years of operation. It became known as the Pollinator, Scott said, and was designed to look like the living room of the house he owned on Wilkins Avenue. "It was an amazing house that had these Formica walls," he said. "It was done by a famous artist, Regina Fischer, whose work was on the cover of *Life* magazine. When I bought the house, I didn't change anything." The house had a unique square grid wooden ceiling that resembled a drop ceiling and three-color Formica strips along the wall. Saxman made the same design at the Beehive using vinyl and padding material he purchased at an auto supply shop in nearby Homestead.

Mike also contributed another more curious-looking design piece to the new coffeehouse. In an interview conducted the week the South Side location was closing, Dawn Wallhausen said that Saxman was asked by Scott and Steve to create a table with a marble top—or at least a top that resembled marble. What he heard, however, was that they wanted tables made of marbles. As a result, he created a piece with a plexiglass top that was filled with marbles. The look worked so well, Steve said, that they decided to create the entire bar with the same aesthetic. "We drilled holes in the bar, and then we dropped marbles into the holes, and underneath the bar there were these lights that would come up through the marbles," he remembered.

Other works also had unintended consequences for the café.

Michael Monack was better known for his graffiti tag, "Mook." The artist was part of the crew that called itself the Value Krew, or VK, according to Wikipedia. He drew the ire of then–Pittsburgh mayor Tom Murphy for his work, which was often created in hard-to-reach places, like the top of a bridge.

Scott said that once other people noticed the artwork and made the connection to Mook, they, too, started to leave graffiti behind. "That was always a struggle," he said.

Another artist, Hector Casanova Cinderhouse, then only fourteen, created a large mural in the coffeehouse that Kramer said depicted an orgy. The painting was so controversial, Scott said, that when certain Christian groups rented rooms at the coffeehouse, they were forced to cover the mural.

LESLIE DONOVAN WAS PART of the team of employees that opened the new location. She worked as one of its first baristas. A University of Pittsburgh student at the time, she lived in Shadyside and had visited the South Side coffeehouse before the Oakland store opened. "That blew everyone's mind," she said. "That was the craziest thing anyone in Pittsburgh had seen."

Like Valerie Gatchell-Christofel, Donovan remembered the Oakland Beehive as a place where the young and hip both patronized and worked.

Leslie Donovan.
Photograph by Nikole
Boyda McGuinness.

"It was wild," she said. "We were all very, very attractive. You know, fluid relationships happened. Scott and Steve were so cool. Because they owned the business, they seemed so much older, but they were only like five years older than us. We would say, 'You have to party, right?' And they did. I met a lot of people. It was a wild ride."

The original plan was for the Oakland café to be open twenty-four hours a day—like the South Side location—but that idea never worked in the college community. As a result, Scott and Steve, at first, hired a very large staff that Leslie said was pruned, either because employees quit when they didn't get enough hours or staff was laid off. Valerie eventually migrated to the East Carson Street store.

NIKOLE BOYDA MCGUINNESS JOINED Leslie as one of the early employees at the Oakland location. Like Valerie Gatchell-Christofel, she was interviewed by Marla, who was charged with hiring the employees for the new store. And like Valerie, she said that it took some tenacity before she was hired. "After my initial interview, I didn't hear back, and then Steve called and asked if I could come in for an interview, and I was like, 'I already did an interview.' But I went in and got hired, I think because I was passionate about coffee."

Even after meeting with Steve, she didn't start work immediately, she said. "I kept calling and asking, 'When am I going to get on the schedule? When am I going to start working?' I wrote in my journal, 'What's going on? Are they screwing with me?' Eventually, I got on the schedule working weekends and evenings."

Unlike so many others who worked at the Beehive, Nikole had already served coffee as her father's unofficial slinger. "My love of coffee started with my father's coffee. He would have me make him a cup—half a teaspoon of instant coffee, one teaspoon of creamer and two teaspoons of sugar. It smelled delicious," she said. "I would take a sip of it. I loved coffee. I love coffee. I'm still obsessed [with] it."

Before taking the job at the café, Nikole moved to Georgia with a friend. She said they would spend their time at a place called Oxford Books that included

Kings Court, Oakland Beehive. *Photograph provided by Scott Kramer and Steve Zumoff.*

a coffeehouse. She would spend hours there, reading books, journaling and drinking espresso. "I used to go to the coffeehouse. I was fascinated with Beat culture. It was who I wanted to be. That was the lifestyle I wanted," she said.

After Nikole moved back to Pittsburgh, a friend mentioned to her that there was a new coffeehouse on the South Side and that the owners were opening a second location in Oakland.

At eighteen, Nikole was one of the youngest employees at the coffeehouse, and she also worked at the Kinko's next door. As a Penn Hills resident without a car, her father dropped her off and picked her up before and after each shift, a twenty-minute ride each trip.

Nikole, who wasn't going to college at the time, said her young age was a hindrance. "You have to understand, my dad was dropping me off and picking me up. After my shift, when most of the people that worked or hung out there were going out, I was going back to Penn Hills. I was the only one not living in Oakland and partying and drinking and staying up all night. It was a really lonely time."

Top: John Cusack came by the Beehive, Polaroid in hand. Nikole Boyda McGuinness took the actor's photograph with his camera and kept the picture. *Photograph by Nikole Boyda McGuinness.*

Middle: Cusack's autograph. *Photograph by Nikole Boyda McGuinness.*

Bottom: Cusack took a photograph of Nikole, as well. He used a lighter to create the photograph's effect, pre-Instagram. *Photograph provided by Nikole Boyda McGuinness.*

Left: Nikole was known to dance on a table or two. *Photograph provided by Nikole Boyda McGuinness.*

Right: The *Coffee and Tea* book that employees were required to read and were tested on. *Nicole Boyda McGuinness, private collection; photograph by David Rullo.*

During Nikole's time working the night shift, the Beehive developed its early identity, first as a coffeehouse, then as a coffeehouse that played movies and, finally, as a coffeehouse that played movies that was also home to band concerts and other performances. She remembered poetry readings and an early show by Rusted Root. She already knew the band's drummer and percussionist, who would often come into Kinko's to make flyers for the band's performances. Her boss at the print shop wanted to keep the musician happy. "He would make these huge stacks of flyers and calendars, and I would be like, 'Six cents, please.'"

Particularly enjoyable for Nikole were the company parties that Scott and Steve would throw. She said that the invitation-only events included both employees and customers who were friends with the owners. "They would have everyone come and would lock the doors. They put on movies and music. It was a great time. I remember I danced on a table at one—that's where I started that. I danced on tables for a while."

Nikole became fast friends with Leslie, whom she says she got drunk with for the first time, sharing a bottle of Absolut vodka. Nikole also joined the fraternity and sorority of Beehive regulars who first tried acid during their tenure at the coffeehouse.

Despite the frivolity, Nikole said that Scott and Steve were very sincere about their place in the coffee landscape and took things like the amount of foam on a drink seriously. "The used to say, 'You need to know the difference between this kind of coffee and that kind and be able to tell the customers what they taste like.'" Required reading, she said, was *Coffee and Tea*, by Elin McCoy and John Frederick Walker. One's employment required taking a test after reading the book. Scott remembered the book but thought the requirement of reading it and being tested on it was a product of manager Marla Misch.

Years later, recognizing the time and distance required by her father to drive her back and forth to work and realizing how young she was, she asked her dad why he allowed her to work there. "I couldn't hold you back," he told her. "You would have found it anyways, and I wanted you to experience the world."

RACHEL ASHER SILVER STARTED to hang out at the Oakland Beehive in 1995. Like so many others, she said that once she discovered the coffeehouse, she "pretty much lived there."

When she turned eighteen, Rachel was hired to work at the coffeehouse. Her job was originally a mishmash of different activities. "I learned how to run the movies in Oakland and would pass out flyers—whatever they needed," she said. "During the phase when they were hosting raves and concerts, I worked as a bartender."

A free movie pass that was given to Brian Rose. *Photograph by Brian Rose.*

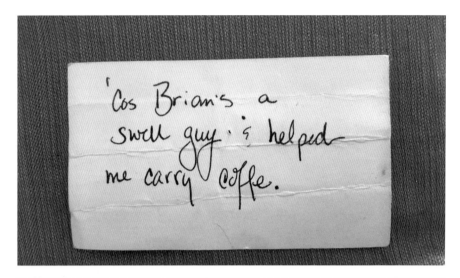

Top: A humorous note explaining why Brian Rose was given a free movie pass. *Photograph by Brian Rose.*

Bottom: An internet hook-up was rented at the Beehive. *Rob Long, private collection; photograph by David Rullo.*

Eventually, Rachel began repairing computers at the Beehive, a skill she picked up while she was a student at the University of Pittsburgh. It was a proficiency that became particularly useful when the Beehive began renting internet time by the hour. She helped Scott and Steve develop a system in which they could print out codes that gave people computer access for a specified amount of time. "It was very successful," she said. "People were desperate to have computers, and wi-fi was really expensive at that point."

Rachel said that she and Steve bonded as they ran cables for the computers not just at the Beehive but also at what was then the Tiki Lounge.

Her job continued to evolve, she said, as the technology changed, and she added computers and wireless connections.

The experience paid off. Rachel started her own business, offering tech support to other stores and bars like the Culture Shop and the Smiling Moose.

THE TWO BEEHIVE LOCATIONS would eventually fall into symmetry, exchanging ideas, employees and even customers—but that didn't mean the new kid on the block didn't find ways to harass its big brother.

An employee at the South Side Beehive might have made their way to the fax machine to find a note that read, "ATTN MARLA & CRONIES YOU SUCK, LOVE OAKLAND." Another note read, "Newsflash South Side Beehive Burns in Hell."

It was, of course, all in good fun, but it helped create a friendly rivalry between the two locations.

EARLY ON, THE OAKLAND Beehive tended to lean on the type of activities and events that were popular at the first location.

Downstairs, those who were looking for a quick coffee before dashing to class or work could find a seat either inside or at a table on the sidewalk. Upstairs, students could linger and study. The larger of the two rooms on the second floor was used for typical coffeehouse events: poetry readings and acoustic music performances. The first floor was also home to the building's original movie theater. It retained the original seating and had a few added couches, connecting the coffeehouse theme to the room.

While the original King's Theater grew its following on screenings of the *Rocky Horror Picture Show* and first-run features, the newly renovated theater would come to be known for its showing of cult and arthouse films, as well as second-run movies. That decision, Scott said, wasn't simply based on

Stickers featuring the Beehive's logo. *Scott Kramer and Steve Zumoff, private collection.*

Left: A place to study and grab a cup of coffee—what more could a college student want? *Scott Kramer and Steve Zumoff, private collection.*

Right: A Jewish film festival program screened at the Beehive, February 1997. *Scott Kramer and Steve Zumoff, private collection.*

economics. The previous owners of the building still had several theaters around town and didn't want to see their former Oakland location cut into their business, he said. As a result, it was hard for the Beehive to show first-run films.

Despite the difficulties of obtaining big films for premiers, Steve remembers the coffeehouse scoring a few wins. "One first-run film that was big for us was *Kids*. Another was *Clerks*, because no one wanted to touch it. They were like, 'What's this black and white film with the language and just two guys talking?'" he remembered with a laugh.

Steve said that despite the challenges, they found ways to make the theater work. For instance, he said, they often did theme nights, which were tougher in the day of analogue films. If he asked distributors for several films from the '70s for a particular night, they would have to search them out and find reels in which the film had begun to disintegrate. "Now, it's easy, because everything is digital," he said. "Back then, they would send us something, and sometimes, the entire film would be red."

No matter the titles being shown at the theater, Steve said that some movie geeks came for the "old-time" feel of the theater, noting that the theater and its equipment were aged.

Sometimes, finding ways to make things work presented opportunities that wouldn't have been possible had the Beehive achieved its goal of showing first-run films. Scott remembered the time Russ Meyer, known for underground classics like *Faster, Pussycat! Kill! Kill!* and *Vixen* made an appearance at the theater. "Most directors don't own their films, but he does," Scott said. "He went on tour with them. Me and Steve got to go to dinner with him while he was in Pittsburgh and hang out with him."

MARK CHOI WORKED AS the coffeehouse's projectionist and was also a jack of all trades quasi-manager who ran sound when the coffeehouse hosted a band. He even worked behind the counter as a barista when needed.

Choi had earned his stripes in Pittsburgh's underground art and alternative music scene pre-Beehive. In the late '80s, he was one of the owners of the Sonic Temple in Wilkinsburg, a once prosperous borough adjacent to the city that had fallen on hard times after the collapse of the steel mills. As a result, it had cheap real estate, like the former Masonic temple that found life as a nightclub.

The Sonic Temple played host to a bevy of underground acts, mainly due to one of Choi's co-owners, Manny Theiner, and his taste in music. A partial list of the club's acts includes My Life with the Thrill Kill Kult, Fugazi, White Zombie and Sick of It All. The show that most continue to talk about, however, took place on July 9, 1989, and featured a still little-known, three-piece act from Seattle: Nirvana. The soon-to-be grunge legends even spent the night on Choi's couch following the show. "That was my birthday party," Choi remembered. "Nirvana played my birthday party."

Mark started working as the theater's projectionist when one of his friends quit after a fight with Scott. "We had two projectors, and you had to switch between them. You had to be able to time the reels right so that you didn't have any breaks in the film," he recalled. "I ended up becoming the head projectionist and did that for a while, which got me from behind the counter."

Mark said that, eventually, the theater obtained a modern "platter" system that allowed all the reels of film to be spliced together, meaning the counter managers could run the movies. This eliminated the need for a full-time projectionist.

Working as a projectionist meant that he spent a lot of time at the coffeehouse, because as Steve mentioned, many of the films were in poor condition. "Especially with third- and fourth-run movies, the prints were in bad shape. Every now and then, they'd break in the middle. I would hear it and have to run upstairs and splice out the broken or burnt part really quick and try to cue it up to the right spot with everyone swearing and being pissed off," he said.

Michael Laughlin was a student at the University of Pittsburgh in 1991. For him, the Oakland Beehive was a movie theater first, and he appreciated the mix of titles available, including the Steven Segal vehicle *Under Siege* and Richard Linklater's *Dazed and Confused*. Of particular note for Laughlin was a midnight showing of *Saturday Night Fever*. He said that the coffeehouse was selling merchandise to accompany the screening, something that fit in with

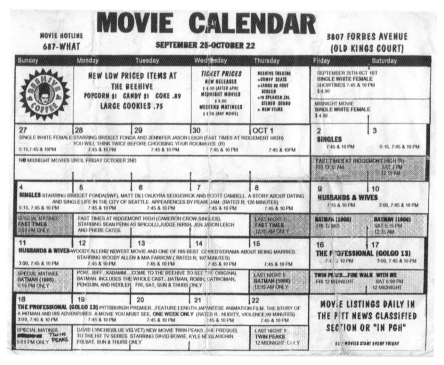

A calendar of movies that were showing at the Oakland Beehive. The films ranged from a Woody Allen movie to Cameron Crowe's grunge title *Singles*. *Scott Kramer and Steve Zumoff, private collection.*

Scott's modus operandi—figuring out ways to not let an opportunity pass and to make a buck wherever possible.

Michael credits the Beehive with changing his musical tastes through one film he saw at the theater. "I saw *Velvet Goldmine*, and it really turned me into a fan of glam rock. I bought the soundtrack and that led me to buying CDs of bands like the New York Dolls and the Stooges," he said. "I bought Barney Hoskyn's book about glam, which mentioned the book *Please Kill Me!* about punk rock. That's what got me into underground music."

THE LARGER SPACE AND multiple rooms allowed the owners to try out different events the South Side Beehive was simply too small to accommodate.

Steve was a pinball fan and had several games at the South Side location. He soon partnered with Kevin Martin and several other people to create a league and held various competitions in the city. The first location they tried was the Oakland Beehive. The tournament proved so popular that the Beehive couldn't accommodate the number of games needed or the large crowds that began attending the competition. So, they eventually moved out of the coffeehouse, but games continued to be featured at the Oakland location.

A pinball tournament flyer. *Scott Kramer and Steve Zumoff, private collection.*

In fact, Scott and Steve even employed a Pittsburgh architect, Rob Indovina, to build a private room on the second floor for pinball games. It was designed so that the sound coming from the room would be deadened and not affect those enjoying the movies or a conversation with friends. "He was a friend of Dale Lazar," Steve said in reference to the Beehive's pinball supplier. "He designed this sort of cube made out of polyurethane particle board with all those little grooves and stuff in it. It was pretty fancy and the only pinball room he designed, I think."

While pinball proved to be a winner, other ideas the pair tried at the location didn't fare so well.

Science Fiction Movie Marathon flyer, Oakland Beehive. *Scott Kramer and Steve Zumoff, private collection.*

Scott had heard that science fiction festivals were becoming popular across the country and that one in Columbus, Ohio, had already proven to be very successful. He quickly planned a similar event for the Beehive. "I put it together for February. It was a complete flop. We spent a lot of money, but it snowed. There was a snowstorm. It was supposed to be a twenty-four-hour festival. It bombed."

At one point, the pair even rented space to an Israeli chef who served Middle Eastern vegetarian food. "He had a cooler and gave us a percentage. That didn't work so well," Kramer said.

An '80s night, which was moved to the Beehive after the Upstage, a popular Oakland location, closed, was more successful. "We moved it to our place without skipping a beat," Scott remembered. "We had quarter drafts on Monday nights, like they did. Instantly, we had a new clientele. It was probably our biggest night."

Eventually, even raves were added to the coffeehouse's regular events, and alcohol was sold there, something that was unavailable to the South Side location in its first decade.

Live shows featuring national acts were soon added to the mix of offerings at the coffeehouse. A partial list of the musicians and bands that performed there includes the Jesus Lizard, Neutral Milk Hotel, Jerry Cantrell, Lizzy Borden, Nelly Furtado, Overkill and Guided by Voices. Scott said that Furtado might have been one of the larger shows at the café. "It was completely sold out. When we booked her, there wasn't any interest, and then she had a hit and people came from all over. We had more than six hundred people there—they were just crammed in. If it had been six months before, no one would have shown up," he said.

When guitar virtuoso Yngwie Malmsteen played the café, Scott remembered having a neighborhood mainstay, who hung flyers for the café, drive Malmsteen's wife, who spoke little English, around town so she could look for a laptop, something new at the time. "'Scott, can you help me find a com-pu-ter,' she said in a thick I think Italian accent," he recalled. "This guy drove her around, but he wasn't a computer guy."

What endeared the Beehive crew to Malmsteen, though, had less to do with the owners' willingness to go the extra mile for his wife and was instead based on a decision Steve made before the guitar player arrived at the venue. "We'd been told that he had been pissed off when he got to a show and there weren't enough speakers," Scott said. "Steve said, 'Let's get a million speakers so there will be a wall of amps when he gets here.' We wanted to make him want to come back, because we were trying to build our clientele."

A menu showing the alcoholic drinks available at the South Side location once it obtained its liquor license. *Scott Kramer and Steve Zumoff private collection.*

OTHER EXPERIENCES AT THE Oakland location weren't as familiar as rock shows or movies.

Leslie Donovan recalled the ramen noodle wrestling. "There was a kiddie pool that they filled with noodles and had people wrestle in it," she said. Mark Hanneman said the idea for the event was his and that Phat Man Dee was a willing partner. Another experience he created was a show similar to *The Gong Show.*

He and Man Dee were living together at Hellrose Place at the time. Mark said that he would just shout out one crazy idea after another until the pair agreed that a concept was worth considering. They even ported some of the events to the Lava Lounge on East Carson Street, but Mark had his eye on an even larger picture. "For a while, I had the idea that I was going to create several club events and try to tour around to different cities," he said. "It just never really came together far enough."

THE UNUSUAL EVENTS MIGHT have helped to create a scene at the coffeehouse, but it was the addition of the Pollinator that eventually allowed the Oakland Beehive to turn a profit.

Scott said in its last year of operation, the café, which had been running at a deficit, finally made $60,000. Until that point, the success of the South Side Beehive subsidized the second location.

An interior shot of the Oakland Beehive. *Photograph provided by Scott Kramer and Steve Zumoff.*

The combination of alcohol, caffeine and music led Scott and Steve to gamble on another Gen X novelty that hadn't been attempted at other cafes: raves. To do that, they relied on a Pitt student and Beehive employee, Tony Banh.

Banh was a pre-med student at Pitt and a member of Scott Kramer's former fraternity, Pi Lamda Phi. He said that he had run various social events for both his high school and fraternity. He is now a

Pollinator Lounge door. *Photograph by Kelly Day.*

production manager at various music festivals in California. At the time, however, like Donovan, he was simply one of the original employees who was hired to work at the coffeehouse.

Despite his father having owned a coffeehouse in his native Vietnam, Tony was unfamiliar with espresso and cappuccino drinks. In fact, he had never tried one, because French drip–style brew was popular in the Southeast Asian country. So, as part of his training, Tony spent time learning about different coffees and their flavor profiles. What he did know about, though, were desserts. He remembered that both the cheesecakes and pastries served, as well as the mocha syrup made, at the Oakland Beehive were high-end and unique.

It was Tony, who had already been hosting raves at the nightclub Soba, which was owned by the local Big Burrito group, who realized that the Beehive's alcohol license was not limited to a particular room, which meant libations could be served anywhere in the building. "I met with Scott and Steve, and we had this secret plan to end what was happening at Soba and bring it to the Beehive," he said.

Intrigued by the theater and excited about the possibility of creating a scene, Tony said he and a partner brought in twenty thousand watts' worth of sound equipment and lighting gear for the raves and named the Wednesday night events "Spawn." "We started the first week of September 1999, and it ran through 2001," he said. "We were bringing headline electronic acts and were kind of before our time. Back then, the concert industry wasn't what it is today."

Tony said that the raves were hits immediately, selling out the location, mainly because the Beehive had the right environment and vibes: a large, open theater that house and drum and bass music sounded good in, plus a progressive clientele that created a good base. "We put in these big chain link

Was Scott a Pittsburgh angel? *Photograph by David Grim.*

fences, separating the over-twenty-one crowd from the underaged crowd—who we let in from the backside so they could get to the dance floor—and we stamped everyone's hands and extended the barista section, making a large bar section. That changed the venue, turning the Beehive into an actual theater," he said.

IT WASN'T SIMPLY THE college community and Gen Xers who found a safe place in the Beehive's two locations. The coffeehouse was a meeting place for an almost forgotten slice of Americana: carnie culture.

8

I'M A FREAK, I'M A GEEK,
I BITE THE BEAK

Dave Gruen, also known as "Dave Apocalypse" and "Slippy the Clown," came from circus folk. Gruen's father, who performed as a clown, emceed at various variety shows and had his own puppet company when David was a child, and he was a link to a previous generation of performers. He said:

> *I'm probably one of the only people my age who know what a funny girl is—that was a female comedian—which was considered a dirty job that a woman wouldn't do. I saw a few of them. I saw the last of the burlesque dancers. I'd go out with my dad's puppet company, and we would do anything from children's parties to be the entertainment of the month at a VA hospital. The lineup would be my dad singing a couple of songs, introducing some aging burlesque dancers and us doing a kid's puppet show. It was bizarre.*

This helped Dave develop an interest in the type of acts that populated the sideshows that traveled from town to town, performing night after night in dusty carnivals and on the side of remote roads. They were the type of shows that were just as likely to feature a magician as they were Siamese twins and other typical sideshow attractions.

By the time the Beehive opened, sideshows had been cast off by most major circus promoters, who focused instead on highwire acts and animal feats. The types of freaks and geeks who interested Dave had been relegated

Circus Apocalypse performs at the Beehive. *Photograph provided by Scott Kramer and Steve Zumoff.*

to Coney Island and the occasional state fair. This, however, didn't blunt his interest.

As a child, Dave taught himself a number of acts, including fire eating, clowning and getting out of straitjackets. Lest one think Dave was interested in these acts merely as novelties, it should be noted that it was after being committed to a mental hospital for a brief period in the first grade and witnessing another child being secured in a straitjacket that he vowed to learn the art of getting out of the restraints.

Though the Beehive existed as a place for those who lived outside of the margins of straight society, Dave was a step beyond the typical artists, musicians and college kids who populated the coffeehouse.

After a stint in the army and then spending some time doing private military work, Dave moved to the South Side and took his place among many of the early adaptors who were living in Hellrose Place. He first worked in a beansprout facility that was located in the basement of the Brew House.

His look was pure carnie, which he said was extremely bizarre for many of the old-timers who lived in the neighborhood with their families.

Eventually, he became accepted as a part of the community and credits a neighbor with helping him cement the idea of starting "Circus Apocalypse."

Dave was practicing eating fire in his apartment's backyard when a neighbor noticed him and said he should be performing. It hadn't occurred to him that others might be interested in what he considered a hobby. "I thought it was just one more geeky thing I did that no one would care about," he said.

Dave enlisted Beehive regular and musician Brian Cummings and Jackie Walker to join him, and he was soon promoting what would come to be known as "Circus Apocalypse." Brian, Dave explained, was his insector, or, in layman's terms, someone who ate bugs. Jackie, who he called his partner in the early days, was his fire eater. "As any good promoter will tell you," he noted with a laugh, "when you think of something to do, you don't do it, you find other idiots to do it for you."

The troupe's first performance was held at the Beehive, where Dave was working as a janitor. "That was great. It was all our friends, but also, most people had never seen that. We were at the tail end of people who were old enough to remember sideshows, so it was either something they saw as a kid or something they had never seen." The show was a resounding success, most likely, Dave said, for two reasons. The first was that entertainment choices had become stagnant. "It was either some form of a rock band or, at best, some kind of performance art, throwing spaghetti and rolling around a bar. Some of that was very good. I had a good time rolling around a bar. It just wasn't what we were doing," he offered. The other reason, he said, was because it's easy to be the best at something when you're the first.

That sense of novelty carried the act far, allowing it to perform in places it would not be able to today.

Fire, sparks from grinders and other dangerous byproducts of the circus were part of the act in crammed bars and clubs, simply because no one told the performers they could not do it. The act, Dave said, was most likely responsible for the "no fire" clause in bars across the region, which was instigated after the group almost burned down a bar in New York during a performance.

Dave named the act Circus Apocalypse. It was because of the act's name that he was dubbed "Dave Apocalypse." A news article inadvertently called him that, not realizing "Apocalypse" wasn't his last name.

Eventually, Cummings was replaced by Andrew Laswell when the former came to a show hungover and without the necessary drive to eat his allotment of bugs. Laswell both lived with Dave at Hellrose Place and worked with him as a janitor at the Beehive. The two were so close, Dave noted, that they were often mistaken for a couple, as they would refer to each other as their "partner."

"The Insector"
shows his skills.
*Photograph provided
by Scott Kramer and
Steve Zumoff.*

Andrew said that his repertoire began to grow shortly after joining Circus Apocalypse. He graduated from eating bugs to doing straitjacket escapes and juggling fire, as well as piercing tricks and lip stitching. "We use sixteen-gauge surgical steel piercing needles, super sharp, and then we glue fishing line in the back of it. We do three piercings, three stitches," he said.

The circus, Laswell said, played pot festivals in Ohio and shows at the Beehive, Dee's and the Serbian Club, as well as anywhere else that would take them. He said that Dave was ambitious and was constantly on the lookout for work.

It was due to a show at Club Nine in the Strip District that the circus got what was perhaps its biggest break: opening for industrial supergroup Pigface in 1995 while the band promoted its album *Feels Like Heaven, Sounds Like Shit*.

As Laswell explained it, the bar double-booked the circus and one of Atkin's bands. "I was like, "Nobody told me. I want my seventy-five dollars,'" he said. "Martin and I discussed it, and he was very gracious. And then Curse Mackey, lead singer for the band Evil Mothers, was like, 'This is great. I have a song that goes, 'I'm a freak. I'm a geek. I bite the beak.'" So, throughout the night, we did three things on the stage, and then we got a call a few months later from Martin asking if we wanted to go on tour.'"

Atkin presented the circus with a choice: get paid for the gigs they performed in the United States or go on tour sans payment, travel to Europe with the band and have their expenses picked up by Atkin's label. Laswell and Dave chose the money.

Of particular note for Andrew was the opportunity the troupe had to perform in Chicago, Pigface's hometown, twice in one day.

The tour, he said, was the start of a lifelong friendship between the two groups. "When Dave moved to California and Pigface was there, he would show up. The same with me when they were in Pittsburgh," he said.

Eventually, Dave had opportunities to join other, larger shows. The allure of performance wasn't enough to keep him in the circus business full time after he met his future wife and followed her to San Francisco, a city he stayed in for several years before he moved back to Pittsburgh and continued to produce shows.

Andrew and Dave joined other circuses during their time working together, including New York's Bindlestiff Family Circus and Circus Ridiculous, a California act Dave Gruen called a "punk rock sideshow." Dave said the three circuses even performed together at one point, producing a seven-hour show in the theater at the Oakland Beehive.

Several other of the coffeehouse's regulars also worked with Dave over the years, including Joyce Bobincheck.

IN THE EARLY '90s, Joyce was a recent Art Institute of Pittsburgh graduate living on the South Side. The Beehive, she said, provided her a place to get her morning coffee, blend in and meet other artists who were living in the neighborhood.

Joyce studied dance as a child. After earning an associate degree in videography—and with her hopes of finding a job as an audio producer dwindling—she decided to pick the art form back up. Instead of the typical tap and ballet that so many young girls start with, she decided to try belly dancing.

It wasn't long after beginning lessons that she met David and Andrew at the coffeehouse. She said that she was soon dating Andrew, which led to her performing in the circus. "They taught me to eat fire," she remembered. "One day, Andrew brought me to see a belly dancer troupe, and I was like, 'That's it.'"

The idea of putting the two skills together was hers, she said, but she credits David and Andrew for allowing her to do what she felt was right. "They taught me a bunch of things,

Circus Apocalypse flyer. *Photograph by Brian Rose.*

but we didn't talk too much about it," she said. "It wasn't something they wanted to do. They had enough other things going on."

When asked how a young woman who had never eaten fire before felt comfortable creating an act that involved not only swallowing fire but also dancing with it, Joyce said, in the end, it was simply about control and the knowledge that she was good at it.

She also said that when she started, belly dancing had yet to make an impact on the East Coast and in Pittsburgh. "It still felt like you were doing something original," Joyce offered. Her act, she said, was different from what David and Andrew were doing, which was a more in-your-face type of performing. Her performance, she said, was more sensual. "With them, it was like, 'This is kind of scary. I'm a little scared right now.' I didn't want people to feel like I was coming at them, because that's what they had the other two doing," she said.

Like many tales about the Beehive and the South Side in the '90s, Joyce's story includes Phat Man Dee. Joyce said the performer took her on the road when she traveled to San Francisco with a traveling troupe that Man Dee had convinced to come along. The energy, she said, was infectious and something she really enjoyed. In the end, Joyce said she enjoyed the trip but was happy when she came back home and decided to stay "off the dirty road."

Once back, Joyce continued to perform, even after David moved to California and she and Andrew were no longer a couple. She remembers her last performance with Laswell being particularly poignant. "We did a show at Metropol. We went on and did fire on a rotating stage, and 'Closer' by Nine Inch Nails came on. I was like, 'This is my song.' And he said, 'This is your last song. Leave everyone talking.'"

NOW A RESPECTED JAZZ singer in Pittsburgh and former member of the Bull Seal Collective, Phat Man Dee received her stage name from Dave in his role as ringleader of the circus. He called her "Mistah Sistah Phat Man Dee."

The performer told the *Pittsburgh Post-Gazette* that she wasn't thrilled with the name at first. "It just stuck," she said. "I didn't really like it, actually."

Phat Man Dee's Bull Seal Collective partner Damon Griffith also played a part in the circus—or at least his daughter did. "His daughter was at a show, and we put a rubber clown mask on her," Dave remembered. "Somehow, she kept it on all night. We told everyone from out of town that she was a drunk midget. Everyone believed us. She tipped over, she couldn't talk, she fell asleep."

Dave said that the '90s lent itself to different types of performers and artists engaging with each other, working to produce something unique. "The economy was in the toilet for a while. Gen X still had some of that trickle down, so to speak, running with the baby boomer's wealth. There was a lot of excess. There were excess apartments, so you could find cheap rent. There was excess shit, so you got excess shit. 'OK, we'll make some art out of it,'" he said. "It might not be good art, but it will be art." In fact, from some of the excess materials Dave found during his time working as a janitor at the Beehive, he fashioned a flying lobster and hung it above the cash register. The sculpture remained there until the Beehive closed.

TODAY, DAVID STILL PERFORMS, mostly as Slippy the Clown. He puts shows on wherever he can—literally. He said he does both kids' parties and adult sex parties. "Mostly, it's the same show—just without the cussing, and I don't make the balloon animals out of condoms. Other than that, it's the same show," he noted.

He has also bought a tent and is beginning to consider putting on larger shows. The city, he said, has enough talent, and there hasn't been a real circus since the Shrine Circus visited almost a decade ago.

CIRCUS APOCALYPSE, DAVID SAID, is a link in the long chain of circus performers who have Pittsburgh connections. The fact that the city is only a twenty-four-hour drive from other locations made it desirable for performers. "Pittsburgh was one of the main hubs of the vaudeville scene," he explained, saying that Daisy and Violet Hilton, cojoined twins who were sideshow attractions, retired in the city, and Houdini did his suspended straitjacket routine from the former Nixon Hotel, now the August Wilson Center. It was also the last spot on the Ringling Bros. Circus's two-year season, David said, because it was close enough to New York and had ample transportation opportunities for those heading to other destinations at the end of the run.

"PITTSBURGH CIRCUS HISTORY IS pretty fucking weird," said Jason Kirin. Kirin is the owner of the Pittsburgh Circus Arts Collaborative and a former Beehive regular.

Kirin noted that Grady Franklin Stiles Jr., better known as "the Lobster Boy," lived in Pittsburgh. One of the original "circus freaks," Stiles suffered from ectrodactyly, in which a person's fingers and toes are fused together to form claw-like extremities. According to Wikipedia, in 1978, Stiles murdered his daughter's fiancé and was sentenced to house arrest and probation.

The peculiarities of Stiles's life don't end there. His first wife, Mary Teresa, left him for Harry Glenn Newman, another circus freak billed as the "Smallest Man in the World." The two were remarried, and in 1992, Teresa, along with her son from a previous marriage, hired sideshow performer Chris Wyant to kill Stiles. All three were found guilty for their roles in their crime.

KIRIN'S FORAY INTO THE world of sideshow and circus performing began after he saw a juggler at Monroeville Mall as a child and decided to learn the skill. Juggling became something he did as a form of escape during his teenage years and into his twenties.

It was an Alan Watts lecture in 2017 that changed Kirin's mindset. "He asked, 'What would you do if money were no obstacle? Do that thing, and money will follow.'" Jason's answer was, "I want to go to the park, get high and juggle all day." Amazingly, his wife gave him the green light to pursue his dream.

It was after Kirin started to follow his bliss that an entertainment company hired him to work at circus weddings, something new that they were beginning to offer. One thing led to another, and Jason eventually bought the Pittsburgh Circus Arts Collaborative, a company started by another performer. "The weddings are still the most important thing to me," he said, noting that the last ceremony they performed was at Mr. Small's Theater, a former church in Millvale located about ten minutes north of the city and owned by former Rusted Root member Liz Berlin. "It was profound. We were able to get everyone in the courtyard with the fire breathers, and everyone in the little theater was watching the

Kabarett Vulgare. *Photograph by David Grim.*

contortionist and jugglers. At the same time, we're dismantling the altar and the tables and chairs and setting up an aerial rig. When everyone came in from the outside, the aerialists dropped from the ceiling," he said.

It's not only traditional circus acts that Jason is interested in, however. He said that the Pittsburgh Circus Arts Collaborative works with the Stolen Stiches Sideshow, as well as Kabarett Vulgare.

CIRCUS ACTS, CARNIVAL PERFORMANCES and sideshows might not be everyone's cup of tea. The Beehive was agile enough to attract those on the fringes of society along with those interested in a pastime that has been captivating American culture for decades: pinball.

9

EXTRA BALL, OR HOW THE BEEHIVE HELPED KICK OFF AN ANALOGUE REVIVAL

Heather Sandmann's favorite game was *Mars Attack*. For Andrew Laswell and Steve Buccigrossi, it was *Medieval Madness*. Joshua Spence, a former barista, remembers "Pinball Steve," an aged greaser from another neighborhood who would come to the coffeehouse every night to play pinball games until close.

Entering the Beehive, one would immediately be hit by the smell of coffee and the sight of oversized art that was painted along the walls. A little farther in, one might notice the mismatched furniture and the people—a mélange of fashion, hairstyles and subcultures. Walk into the back room, though, and one's senses were immediately assaulted by the world of pinball: flappers were heard hitting against metal balls, and games were being nudged or unceremoniously tilted, all blended with the bright lights of the games. Actors from entertainment tie-ins spoke at the same time as sirens announced a free game. Players yelled as a ball was lost or cheered as a multi-ball play was won or a new high score was reached.

For many, the South Side Beehive was more than just a place to grab a quick cappuccino or dessert. They were there for the game. In fact, so popular were the pinball games that lined the back room of the coffeehouse—and so large the Pittsburgh fanbase—that it is not hyperbole to entertain the notion that co-owner Steve Zumoff and a group of friends helped revitalize interest in pinball throughout the Northeast in the 1990s and 2000s.

Steve's interest in the mechanical game that was invented in the 1930s began while he was growing up in Lemoyne, Pennsylvania. Located in Cumberland County across the Susquehanna River from the state capital,

Harrisburg, Lemoyne's population never rose over five thousand. Like most small towns, it had a corner restaurant and market, and when Steve was around nine, he discovered the storefront featured the game *Black Knight*. It was the first title that caught his attention. Today, having played hundreds of titles, he calls *Attack from Mars* his game. What first attracted him to the game, he said, was its analogue nature that required skill, as opposed to the digital video games that were beginning to sweep the nation.

When Steve moved to Pittsburgh, he brought his love of the game with him, playing at Doc's Place in Shadyside. As he and Scott began to plan the aesthetics of their new café, he decided to include pinball. "I wanted the coffeehouse to be the kind of place where I wanted to hang out," he said, "and I like pinball."

Police Force was the first title to be included in the cafe. It was situated in the middle of the coffeehouse and, initially, was just something for Steve or the curious customer to give a go. Eventually, the game became popular, and people waited to play it, as they did for their espressos and desserts on a busy weekend night. When the pair decided to open a previously closed off back room, they filled it with different pinball titles. Steve said they featured six games; Scott is sure there were as many as twelve. Both are certain their Oakland Beehive also included games when it opened.

And while Steve is quick to say he doesn't know if the Beehive was responsible for the game's resurgence in the city, he is quick to add, "Pinball had a big presence in Pittsburgh."

Although Steve might attempt to argue the fact, for most Gen Xers who were frequenting the South Side at the time, the pinball universe started at—or came in contact with—the Beehive's back room. Why this new generation of artists, musicians and bike messengers became attracted to the game is something of a mystery.

By 1990, pinball was at its nadir in the city. There were few locations where the game could still be found. The Smithfield Street News, located beneath an adult bookstore where patrons could rent stalls that played pornographic movies and gay men cruised for dates, had several titles, as did some of the bars and social clubs in each of the city's neighborhoods. Suburban malls that included an arcade might have had one of the games, usually sitting vacant or used as an alternative when the hot new franchise video games were occupied. But for the most part, these games were displaced and forgotten.

Pinball, it seemed, was destined to join the carhop, vinyl albums and rabbit ears on the trash heap.

And yet, the Beehive soon attracted a loyal group of players.

DALE LAZAR WAS A third-generation owner of the B.D. Lazar Company. He joined the company in the late '70s after leaving a career as a teacher. The business was originally a juke box supplier that added pinball games to its offerings, he said.

"The success of pinball at the Beehive," Dale noted, "was remarkable." The Beehive, he said, was likely the most popular venue in the city for pinball and the highest-grossing location in the city.

His relationship with Steve, Dale said, was so unique that none compared during his forty-plus years in the business. "Pinball games are not reliable. There's a lot of service, and Steve was able to do some of that basic service, so he had keys to the games to reduce downtime and increase revenue. Prior to meeting Steve, I never thought I would have given the keys to anybody, but he was so uniquely special and committed and exuded [such] incredible integrity that it was very easy to give him keys to the games," he said. "The games aren't difficult to fix," Steve noted. "They all have the same architecture. If a resistor goes bad on one game, it's likely to be the same resistor on another game. All the mechanical stuff under the theme is the same."

Steve's ability to work on the games meant they spent less time out of service and earned more money than if they had to wait for service by Lazar or someone from his company. Remarkably, because Steve had keys to the games, the relationship between him and Dale evolved to the point that Zumoff would bring Dale his portion of money earned each week. "He would do the collections," Dale remembered, "and he would come to my shop every Friday with bags of coins."

Over the years, the connection between the two grew, and Lazar would often get home later than expected, as he and Steve would share a cup of coffee and talk. So close were the pair that Dale even helped bear the burden of moving the machines from time to time. He said that when the Oakland location opened, he helped carry games up and down the stairs to the second floor—something he would never do today, he said with a laugh.

Steve's creativity, Dale said, helped grow the popularity of pinball in the city, making Pittsburgh ground zero for the game in the United States.

THE SUCCESS OF PINBALL at the Beehive whetted Steve's appetite to increase the visibility of the game in the city. He had already teamed up with a loose group of players to create a few tournaments and events. He met a willing partner in 1993, when he was introduced to Kevin Martin at a pinball expo in Chicago.

Martin was living in the Windy City but would soon move to Pittsburgh to start Pair Networks, a web hosting company. The success of the business allowed him to follow his passion. "I was very much a player. I always have been," Martin said, telling *Inc.* magazine in 2008 that to win at pinball is to triumph over a machine. "It's physical and it's real," he said.

Steve and another associate named Dave Stewart were pushing to create a pinball league, Kevin said. "They originally created the Three Rivers Pinball Association and then, later, the Steel City Pinball Association," he said. "Now, there's a thriving scene with all sorts of leagues and locations. At the time, the two Beehives were the only places to play."

Early on, events were held at the Oakland Beehive. They quickly outgrew the location, however, and were moved to the Best Western Hotel at Parkway Center in Greentree, a suburb west of the city. The space proved to be a hit, drawing people from across the region. "We had the top floor and could fit about twenty-five or thirty machines. The air conditioning couldn't keep up. The elevators were overwhelmed. It was hot and messy, and things were breaking down all the time, but people loved the format. We had a huge turnout and trouble shutting down by 2:00 a.m. or 3:00 a.m. each day," Kevin said.

When Kevin and Steve learned that New York City's Broadway Arcade owner and founder of PAPA, the Professional and Amateur Pinball Association, Steve Epstein was retiring, Martin reached out and bought the league name. Epstein is credited with popularizing the concept of pinball leagues and tournaments, so the name carried a certain weight, on which they were able to build.

By the early 2000s, Kevin saw the advantages of relocating to a new space PAPA would own. He found a forty-thousand-square-foot former warehouse in Scott Township, Pennsylvania, located only a few miles from the Best Western Hotel they were using to host their tournaments. The space had enough room to house his growing collection of games, which, at that point, included more than two hundred titles. In 2004, the PAPA 7 World Pinball Championships were held at the new location.

After successfully christening the new location, floods devastated several businesses, including the new PAPA headquarters. All of the pinball machines were destroyed, as were many of the improvements that had been made to the building after the organization bought it, including the bathrooms and carpeting. But thanks to insurance and a lot of hard work, the space was ready for the following year's championships and had even more games on hand, upping the number of titles to over four hundred.

This page: The PAPA Pinball tournament at the Scott Township location. *Photograph by David Grim.*

The PAPA Pinball tournament at the Scott Township location. *Photograph by David Grim.*

Kevin eventually started a not-for-profit organization called the Replay Foundation, which was dedicated to promoting the preservation, restoration and enjoyment of pinball technology.

Soon, Replay and PAPA outgrew the space they bought in Scott Township and moved the annual tournament, redubbed as an arcade and video game festival, to the David L. Lawrence Convention Center. The center is a 1.5-million-square-foot building located in the heart of downtown that had been refurbished in 2003, becoming the first LEED-certified convention center in North America. It is operated by the Sports and Exhibition Authority of Pittsburgh and Allegheny County.

The pinball festival brought thousands to the city. Kevin said it was the third-largest show presented at the convention center, just following the annual Home Show and Auto Show. "We were really punching above our weight," he said.

COVID changed all that.

The organic growth that started at the Beehive in the '90s and led to the creation of first a league and then an annual convention was stopped in its tracks by the virus. "The first Replay FX event had three thousand people, and four years later, we had thirty thousand. You just can't start that cold again," he said.

In 2020, Replay announced that it would no longer hold events.

Despite no longer holding annual events, the effect of the games on the Beehive's bottom line can't be denied.

Steve said that *Medieval Madness* proved to be the coffeehouse's most popular game. "Over twenty years, we did more than $100,000 in business. It was a lot of money over the years, and that was just one game," he said.

And it seems like many other Pittsburgh entrepreneurs knew a good thing when they saw it. There are now several places to play the game in the city, including Pinball Perfection in the city's North Hills, Pittsburgh Pinball Dojo in Bellevue and Kickback Pinball in Lawrenceville.

In the end, it is the Beehive's customers who helped popularize the game, just as they allowed for the success of the coffeehouse and many of Scott and Steve's future endeavors, including the Lava Lounge, the Tiki Lounge and the Double Wide Grill.

10

THE CUSTOMERS

While the Beehive had ingratiated itself to Pittsburgh's creative community before it even opened, it also found a loyal customer base from those interested in simply having a cup of coffee, indulging in a slice of triple chocolate espresso cheesecake or whiling away the time before attending a show at the City Theatre.

Brian Rose was one of the early adaptors to the Beehive. When he was just seventeen, he moved out of his house after a stint in rehab. He and a friend spent most of their time skateboarding in the Strip District. "One day, we decided to go to the Beehive because we had heard about it from some people. It was magical," he said. "It was like one o'clock in the morning, and it was still open, and there were still people there and still things going on. It was like nothing else in Pittsburgh." Rose said the coffeehouse was the kind of place that made you want to become a regular—and if you were a regular, you always had some place to go.

Brian was so moved by the scene that he moved out of the apartment he was staying in and began living out of a backpack, just so he could be closer to the café. "I was pretty broken in a lot of ways," he said, "but the Beehive was the social world I always needed."

In addition to friends, Brian said, the coffeeshop provided a tiered system of customers. New people were always coming in for an experience they thought would be exotic and exciting. "It probably over-fostered my need to be the center of attention," he said. "But it was the right place to do it."

Brian Rose's interview
with Bill O'Driscoll.
*Taken from a video by
Terence Lee.*

BRIAN WASN'T THE ONLY customer from a troubled background who found a
home at the Beehive. Divorced parents who got married too young, latchkey
children responsible for younger siblings—Generation X had a host of
trauma that left scars on the teenagers who were just becoming adults.

Before spending much time at the Beehive's South Side location,
Steve Buccigrossi used to hang out at the Beehive in Oakland when he
accompanied his father, who worked at the University of Pittsburgh. He
spent his days exploring not only the Carnegie Library but also the clothing
and music stores along Forbes Avenue. Like the South Side, he said, the
college neighborhood had a burgeoning counterculture community. "I felt
more comfortable around people like that," he said. "I had a real short
childhood and found it hard to relate to kids in the suburbs and what they
were doing with their lives."

That inability to relate might have been due to Steve's family situation.
His father was hit by a drunk driver and suffered brain damage. His mother
left. Steve stayed with his father, but he had to mature quickly, as he was soon
responsible for helping with many of the daily responsibilities in their home.
This also might explain some of his troubles he had in high school. Steve
was expelled for a period from his North Hills high school, which meant
he had more time to spend exploring the streets of different Pittsburgh
neighborhoods. It also led to him hanging out with people older than himself,
since they were the ones who were out during the day when he normally
would have been in school. "The potential for all kinds of trouble existed,"
he said. "But people looked out for me in a way. They could probably tell I
was going through some shit as a young kid."

Beehive regular Steve Buccigrossi. *Photograph provided by Steve Buccigrossi.*

In time, Steve began hanging out the Oakland Beehive, spending time upstairs, playing pinball.

He said that he soon learned about the Beehive on the South Side and was taken by the location and its regulars after his first visit. "It was like a clubhouse of people like me," he said. "A lot of different ages, misfit-type characters. It really surprised me, because it didn't take me long to generate some rapport with people there."

The coffeehouse, Steve noted, provided a place of escape for people who were going through abuse or trauma, and he said that many, including himself, were dealing with some form of depression without proper treatment. The camaraderie, he said, helped.

And despite the friendships and like-minded individuals at the Beehive, the potential for danger still existed in this urban location. Steve remembered that various gang members and drug dealers often frequented the coffeehouse, as did skinheads, who would troll the location for potential converts.

Even when the danger was close at hand, it sometimes worked out. Steve said that one time, he was robbed at knifepoint outside the Beehive. The

Painting by Steve Buccigrossi. *Photograph provided by Steve Buccigrossi.*

perpetrator sold all of his possessions, but people returned it all to him because of the relationships he had developed.

One of his friends was Scott Kramer, who he saw as a sort of older brother. He said the Beehive owner took him to the movies and an occasional concert, including the Red Hot Chili Peppers. "He would kind of take us way from that environment, even if it was to do something and just chill," he said. "He was beyond rich to us. We were just amazed by his situation and success."

In the end, Steve was able to beat the odds. He graduated from college and now has a successful Airbnb business and paints in his free time.

"There was a mix of vibrant people there," he said thinking back to his time at the Beehive.

FOR SOME, THE BEEHIVE provided a spot to meet disaffected youth, and for others, it was a place to look for solutions.

Michael Reber grew up in Mount Washington, a few minutes away from the South Side, where his grandmother lived. He said he spent time at her house daily, and while he was there, he would frequent the stores on East Carson Street, including Slacker, Groovy and the Culture Shop.

As a child, Michael said, he was as interested in the coffee and pinball inside the Beehive as well as the life outside the café. "I probably spent equal amounts of time outside on Fourteenth Street, playing hacky sack, as I did inside the Beehive, drinking," he remembered.

Michael said he had a fairly stable group of friends who found the coffeehouse to be an accepting environment. So, as an adult working at UPMC Western Psychiatric, when he was looking for a place to host the Youth Outreach Union, a support group for young adults who were in the system, he chose the Beehive. He said Scott and Steve were welcoming to the group. "We had a small budget, so the youth would come, and we'd buy them all a cup of coffee and sit around and talk about what was on everyone's mind," he explained. The group, he said, would meet in one of the rooms off the main café. Scott and Steve's decision to close that space and go back to one room coincided with the state's decision to offer less support for outreach work, so the group was disbanded.

Michael said the Beehive was a community space that he found inspirational. "There were nights people would put on concerts and on the

A Buzz Club card—buy twelve drinks and receive one coffee free. *Scott Kramer and Steve Zumoff, private collection.*

wall was a gallery space featuring local artists. I purchased some art there. It was definitely a smorgasbord of everything you could think of. It wasn't just a coffee shop," he offered. "It was a community coffee shop. There was a community of folk from up and down the South Side and a network for artists."

A flyer celebrating the Beehive's twenty-fifth anniversary. *Photograph by David Rullo.*

XAVIER EVANS CARRIER BEGAN coming to the Beehive as a teenager. Despite being several years younger than many at the coffeehouse, he said he built relationships there that have lasted.

The café was home to two different scenes when Xavier first started visiting it on a regular basis: grunge and art. It was the art scene that was particularly important to him, especially as a student at CAPA, Pittsburgh's Creative and Performing Arts High School. "It was perfect to be able to go up to the older people, like Rich Bach or loads of other people, and be like, 'OK, what's your thing? I've got this thing.' Half the time, they'd be like, 'We don't have time for you.' Other times, they'd be like, 'We'll give him an idea and see what he does for it.'"

Xavier has taken those early inspirations and channeled them into his professional life. He is a potter at Zotter the Potter.

But wasn't only art that attracted him to the café. Xavier spent time playing *Magic: The Gathering* and pinball at the coffeehouse. Later, he would join Steve at a secret room above the Double Wide Grill, where they would play pinball together. He also joined in games of chess, which he said was a lot of fun—until people began bringing in counters, turning an enjoyable way to spend some time into something more competitive. "Everyone got so serious. I was like, 'I don't want to play this anymore; you've killed it.'"

Taken by the idea of the Beehive and his love of the coffeehouse culture, Xavier became part owner of another short-lived coffeehouse on the South Side, Interstellar. Fortunately, he said, he became an investor at seventeen, which meant that when the coffeehouse closed, he was able to write off the bad idea in his taxes.

DENNIS MITCHELL SUFFERS FROM the genetic disorder corpus callosum, meaning the bundle of nerves that connect the left and right hemispheres of his brain is either missing or partially missing. He spent time at the Beehive in his youth, but when his mother was diagnosed with terminal cancer, he became a regular there. It was a place, he said, where he could find an escape. "I took my computer and just started hanging out there every day."

Dennis said one particular moment stuck out in his mind that exemplified the type of community that existed at the coffeehouse. "This guy came in and said, 'They let retards in here,' pointing at me.'" The outsider was someone from Dennis's neighborhood who knew of his disorder. A Beehive patron stood up and castigated the person. When the person who issued the insult threatened the second customer, a third stood up to defend him. Not deterred, the aggressor said he would fight both of them, issuing the rhetorical question, "Who's going to back you up? Where's your army?"

"Everybody in the Beehive stood up and said, 'We're his army.' The guy that made the comment hadn't ordered anything yet, and he left," Dennis remembered.

A budding filmmaker, Dennis said the Beehive helped him weather not only the death of his mother but also the passing his father a year later.

It wasn't only the customers with whom Dennis found community. He remembered a time when he went to see *Jurassic World* with a barista who knew of his interest in films.

He's still friends with those he met during his time at the coffeehouse and keeps up these relationships on various social media sites, but Dennis said he continues to miss the Beehive and thinks about it every day.

Beehive swag. *Photograph by Nicole Boyda McGuinness.*

FOR OTHERS, THE COFFEEHOUSE provided a place for them to see the latest fashions, and some of the neighboring stores offered them the chance to buy clothing and accessories to mirror those trends.

Heather Sandmann grew up in a small town in Pittsburgh's South Hills suburbs. After high school, she moved to the city and began working at

Slacker next door to the Beehive. "When I went to the Beehive, that was the first time I ever had a latte," she said. "I didn't know what they were. I was kind of sheltered, so it was good to get me out of my shell."

Like many who were new to the South Side, Sandmann was pleasantly surprised by the stores and products she found on East Carson Street, saying that what first attracted her to Slacker were the store's cosmetics and clothing, which was so different from what was available at suburban malls like South Hills Village. "They had Urban Decay, and I went nuts for that. They had nail polish that I loved and hair dye that I used. And they had some of the coolest clothing. Dollhouse was a label that they had," she said.

Before the days of online shopping, Heather said there were few options for buying trendy or artistic items and that when she moved to the city, the South Side was the place she came to shop.

Working at Slacker, next door to the Beehive, presented Heather an opportunity to get to know customers of both stores. She said they shared a large customer base.

After taking in all of the neighborhood's culture that she could, Heather decided to move to California, inspired by Scott and Steve's cross-country trip. "It was good to have some of that counterculture," she said. "When I moved, I did the whole Kerouac Big Sur–Bixby Ridge on the California coast kind of thing."

MEGAN GRABOWSKI GREW UP in Dormont, Pennsylvania, the first community outside of the city in what is known as the South Hills. She attended a Catholic school and spent her downtime, like many teenagers, visiting the local shopping mall.

She learned about the Beehive almost a year after it opened, saying that it took some time for word of the coffeehouse to make it outside of the city. The coffeehouse, she said, was where you went to see "the people who had the guts to dress the way you wanted to dress, wear their hair the way you wanted to wear your hair, but maybe, growing up in the suburbs, you were a little hesitant to make that move." The café provided Megan with positive affirmation that there were others like her who wanted to look the way the people in *Rolling Stone* and the movies did. Or perhaps it was proof that there were others who were not interested in dressing the way she saw others dressing in her hometown, less than ten minutes from the Beehive—Penguins jerseys, B.U.M. Equipment shirts and gold chains. At the Beehive, she found others who were interested in the same pop culture she was exploring: the

Smiths and Depeche Mode, *120 Minutes* on MTV and programs like *Liquid Television*, which featured interesting and cutting-edge animation.

Before finding the coffeehouse, "I was a little bit of an outsider," she said.

As Megan matured, so did her choice of drinks—moving from sweet Italian sodas to coffee with a little cream and a lot of sugar and then, finally, to black coffee. And as she started taking classes at Carlow College, she moved from the Beehive's South Side to its Oakland location.

The café's second location offered concerts by bands Megan was interested in, as well as movies and, just as importantly to the budding writer, poetry readings. "As I was going to school for writing and writing poetry, it became even more important for me to be around other artists," she said.

"The Beehive was the place for artists. I painted a lot, and I drew," Nicole Rieder said when thinking back to what she liked about the coffeehouse. She was dating a musician in the band Half Life at the time and, in addition to the café, she spent time on both the South Side and in Oakland, hanging out and seeing bands like Pittsburgh punk band Anti Flag.

Nicole said that her experience in both neighborhoods began before she was twenty-one, so in theory, she couldn't get into clubs. In reality, after spending her days frequenting thrift shops, art galleries and the Beehive, she would get into bars like the Upstage because she knew the bouncers.

For her prom, Nicole bought jewelry from the long-closed Yesterday News. She also frequently bought things from a vending machine that Scott and Steve had at the Beehive, which contained a variety of odd items not usually available in the machines that normally sold only candy bars and snacks. "I remember I bought my boyfriend tickets to Hatebreed there," she said.

The Beehive was serious about its coffee intake. *Scott Kramer and Steve Zumoff, private collection.*

By the time she was attending classes at Carlow College, Nicole was focused on fashion and music, spending much of her free time at clothing stores or hunting for CDs at Dave's Music Mine. Those times proved valuable to Nicole, who would become an online influencer for plus-size women. She said that she would get upset shopping at a store like the Avalon, where she not only couldn't find clothes to buy but was also unable to sell some of the clothes she had purchased at other locations. "It was really frustrating. I was smaller than I am now, and they would tell me that a size 14 was too big," she said. "It's like the Wild West. If you're a plus-size woman, you have to work harder."

She has even found herself in some of the magazines she used to purchase at Slacker, which has meant a lot to her.

Nicole's friend Michele Joann shopped with her at the various stores, attended concerts at the Oakland coffeehouse and spent time at the Beehive and other late-night spots, like Tom's Diner.

Michele said that it was while she was a student at Point Park that she first started coming to the South Side—and she continued coming into her early twenties, bringing others who worked with her. "It was nice times," she said. "We would go there and smoke cigarettes and get big pots of tea and sit there for hours."

During the early days of the internet, Scott and Steve brought computers into the café. They sold cards that allowed customers to surf the net for set amounts of time. Michele said that was a draw for her when it was still unique for people to have home computers, especially in dorm rooms or college apartments.

Still, it was the physical interactions that mattered to the pair. Nicole said one memory in particular stays with her. At the time, she was still a teenager, living with her parents in Robinson Township, a community approximately half an hour from the Beehive. When her friend turned sixteen, her parents rented a limousine to take the group of friends to the South Side. "I remember going to Eye of Horus and Slacker at its old location. We went to Groovy's and bought He-Man toys out of a little toy pool. Then we went to the Beehive to hang out. It was like a sort of introduction to adulthood," she said.

For others, the Beehive served as a place to while away their teenage years.

Elaina McCullough began frequenting the Beehive because she was under twenty-one and "had nowhere else to hang out." After getting a taste of what could be experienced there, she said she kept going back. "Back then, there was the Summer Street Spectaculars that happened. I had so much fun when I hung out down there," she said.

A whimsical sign soliciting tips.
Scott Kramer and Steve Zumoff, private collection.

The South Hills resident spent so much time at the Beehive that when she was applying for different jobs, she listed the shop's phone number as her own on applications. In fact, she even met her daughter's father at the shop, as he would often be there playing *Magic: The Gathering*.

Elaina's friend Beth Lynn Eicher said that the South Side represented an opportunity to be in a place less commercial than the South Hills and other suburban neighborhoods. "The vibe was definitely different than the Beehive and where it was located. It was a snobby 'Mount Lebanon scene.' People who did have alternative thoughts went to the South Side—it was LGBTQ friendly. Out there, it was like, 'We're better than everybody else,'" she offered.

JOCELYN ORTEGA BEGAN GOING to the Beehive when she was about twelve. She said her reason for initially spending time at the coffeehouse was simple: you could smoke there. And while, by her own admission, Jocelyn spent a lot of time there, she said that she actually made very few purchases. "I probably bought eight things in all the years I was there. I bought a pop or a little snack because I was hungry. I would play pinball in the back. I love pinball," she said. "*Medieval Madness* is still my favorite." She said that she also liked spending time in the courtyard, noting that a lot of shenanigans went on in the lot, beyond the watchful eyes of others.

Unlike those who said the café represented an escape from daily stress, Jocelyn said that she actually got into more than one fight at the Beehive. One occurred as she was leaving the café on East Carson Street. Scared by what she had done, Jocelyn ran away, she

The Beehive courtyard, a favorite place for patrons to hang out or spend a few minutes away from the crowd for whatever reason. *Photograph provided by Scott Kramer and Steve Zumoff.*

said. Several days passed before she was able to gather the courage to return. She probably didn't need to fear repercussions, she said, because when she returned, a customer said to her, "You kicked that girl's ass."

A MORE IDYLLIC MEETING at the coffeehouse occurred between Joe and Penny Stafura, who had their first date at the Beehive. The pair are married now and own a house in the South Side Slopes, a short ride from the former café.

Joe worked on the South Side, first for an advertising company and later with his own business in digital photography. "There wasn't a lot open on East Carson Street. There was Mario's, but I'm really not a drinker, so I started going to the Beehive and eating Curtis's vegetarian food."

Living and working on the South Side, he said, meant that the Beehive often served as a kitchen of sorts.

One of the first experiences Joe remembered having at the café was witnessing ramen noodle wrestling. When he says that he experienced the often-discussed event, he means it. Joe wrestled Phat Man Dee in the kiddie pool holding the noodles. "I had just left my job in corporate America and said, 'I'm really going to blow this out.' So, I went home, put on my three-piece suit and carried my briefcase with some dollar bills in it and went as 'Corporate Evil.' It was a cathartic kind of thing."

That wasn't the only unique experience of which Joe and Penny were a part. The second was at the Oakland Beehive and took place when Joe was entertaining a group of mechanical engineers from California and Boston. "The Beehive had this event, and they were looking for sponsors," he said. "I had just sold my company and had some money, so I figured, 'That sounds like fun. I'll sponsor that.'" The "it" was an exhibition of flame-throwing robots at the Oakland Beehive. "It had to be illegal," Joe said. "Man Dee was in a rotating cage that had fire right under it on stage."

Summarizing the experiences he witnessed during his time at the Beehive, Joe said, "It was a couple of ludicrous years. The '90s had some tough years. Sometimes, it's fun to do some really ludicrous things. I'll tell you, that was a terrific community to do fun things with. There were brilliant, creative people there."

AND WHILE MOST WILL tell you that when they walked through the doors of the Beehive they felt an immediate attraction to the coffeehouse, Kumar Ramanathan is the exception. "My first exposure to the Beehive was the

A framed painting from the Beehive's wall. *Scott Kramer and Steve Zumoff, private collection.*

Oakland location. I went in there, hanging out with some buddies of mine in college, and I was like, 'This place sucks. What am I doing here?'"

He said that as a young person, he had numerous perceptions of what his social circle should look like. The Oakland Beehive did not fit into any of those visions.

That all changed when he ventured to the East Carson Street location.

"It was bizarre, because I thought, 'This is awesome,'" he remembered. He said he would go to the South Side location every day to place chess and hang out with the regulars. "I was just a pretentious asshole," he offered.

The café, he said, didn't foster typical transactional relationships; rather, there were what he called "meaningful punches to the face, filled with humor and a little philosophical discourse."

It wasn't only the Beehive that attracted Kumar's attention. He said that Slacker also served as a source of inspiration. "What the Beehive exposed me to was the world of artistic entrepreneurship and artistic endeavor. I met people wanting to accomplish things in nontraditional ways," he said.

The concentrations of customers who were mostly interested in alternative and Gen X culture changed the areas in which they were located. The character of the neighborhoods evolved, first organically and then in more corporate ways, as East Carson Street and Forbes and Fifth Avenues were gentrified. In the end, it left some of the original patrons feeling angry and displaced.

11

HERE COMES THE NEIGHBORHOOD

Pre-Beehive, the storefronts on East Carson Street catered to the community that existed there. Small grocery stores, delis, butchers, a magic shop and, of course, bars. The street also had several small art galleries and a few independent bookstores.

The customers who began moving into and visiting the neighborhood started a transformation. The South Side first became known as the place to find the city's young art community before it eventually became a victim of its own success. Gentrification and rising rents meant the local entrepreneurs who had spent decades building their business were soon priced out of the community.

When the coffeehouse first opened, though, the local community was unsure what to make of the new generation of people moving into and frequenting their neighborhood.

Julie Rose said there was a tension that initially existed between the two groups. "Some of the people that lived there for a really long time and were used to the way things were were resentful of the parking headaches and all the people that began pulling into the scene that was there," she said.

Circus Apocalypse creator David Gruen said that the mixing of the two cultures was, at first, rife with anxiety. "The joke was a bunch of blue-haired ladies at O'Leary's are complaining about the people moving into the neighborhood with green hair," David said.

The situation began to change when the longtime residents saw what the new group brought to the community. "We didn't trash apartments. Most

The Beehive's façade. *Still taken from a video recorded by Terence Lee.*

of us were decent workers if we got a job. A lot of the people were also the local kids," he said.

In fact, as the neighborhood slowly morphed into a bar and entertainment location, those original homeowners who were hostile toward the original Gen Xers moving in soon found a common enemy in the new, loud, brash and disrespectful "weekenders" who came in to get drunk, urinate in the alleyways, litter and then head home to begin another workweek. "When it started to get popular with people outside of the neighborhood, they thought that wasn't right. We weren't those people roaming the streets looking for stuff to get into," Gruen said.

AS THE LOCALS BEGAN to see the Beehive's customers as a boon to the area and became used to the idea of paying more than fifty cents for a cup of coffee, other stores began to open that catered to the new South Side converts.

Slacker, which opened its doors in September 1991, only six months after the Beehive, influenced the new alternative culture as much as the funky coffeehouse next door. Inspired by Trash and Vaudeville at St. Mark's Place in New York City and reminiscent of SEX, the London boutique opened by Vivienne Westwood and her partner Malcolm McLaren (who would go onto manage the Sex Pistols), Slacker was opened by Randy Przekop and his sister Debbie and was named after the Richard Linklater film.

Above: The Beehive's neighbor, Slacker. *Photograph provided by Scott Kramer and Steve Zumoff.*

Opposite: A flyer advertising the Slacker fashion show at Metropol, another Gen X cultural touchstone no longer in existence. *Scott Kramer and Steve Zumoff, private collection.*

Randy said he was motivated to open a store for the type of person who was considered to be a slacker in the film. Texas writer James L. Haley, in a book of the movie's script, wrote that the term *slacker* refers to a netherworld of "space cadets, goonballs, punk groups, gently aging iconoclasts, coffee shop feminists gone 'round the bend, conspiracy dweebs lurking in used bookstores, artists, anti-artists, and a whole purgatory of other refugees from the world of productive sanity." It was the perfect description of the community that had begun to call the South Side home by the early '90s.

Slacker offered fashion influenced by punk and sex clubs, as well as shoes, jewelry, hair dye, zines and underground magazines. It even rented out cult and underground movies.

The store brought together the neighborhood's disaffected youth and those looking for edgier choices than what could be found in their local malls. It also built a symbiotic relationship with the Beehive, sharing customers and a vision of the world.

Randy, like the Beehive's owners, even opened a second location in Oakland, but he closed the store about a year later, realizing that the siren's call of multiple stores was fool's gold.

Joesph Rembiz managed both locations at one time or another.

1321 EAST CARSON STREET
PITTSBURGH, PA 15203
412.381.3911

SLACKER

lost generation wear

PRESENTS

FASHION SHOW AT

METROPOL
METROPOL
METROPOL

CLOTHES, SHOES, AND JEWELRY **THURSDAY, DEC 19 • 9PM**

A former employee of Joseph Horne, an iconic Pittsburgh department store that competed with Kaufmann's, Joseph was hired part time by Randy in 1992. He became a full-time employee in 1995. When he was first hired, he said, Slacker was still forming its identity. He helped by arranging the purchase of several store fixtures from Horne.

The store, he said, was a sideshow to the Beehive, where he would stop for a cup of coffee but not linger because he wasn't initially part of the same social scene. "People would leave there, wander over, and I'd be a captive audience," he said.

A buzz existed around the South Side location, Joseph said, especially when it first opened, because it was so unique to Pittsburgh and appeared to be super trendy without chasing any particular trend. It was populated with the type of fashion that interested Randy, who, by default, became a tastemaker to the scene.

Sometimes, that worked out, like when he bought T-shirts from Madeline Warholak, a relative of Andy Warhol. "They played off Andy's legacy and had chicken prints and those type of things on them," he said.

Other popular items at the store were the Tish and Snooky hair dye and cosmetics, a New York City line, and big hoop earrings.

Other objects seemed like they would work but proved to be too difficult to sell, like Doc Marten shoes, for example. "There was only one place selling those—the Army Navy Surplus Store downtown. We tried to expand on it, but shoes are a pain," Randy explained. "You have to keep every size in stock, and it ends up taking a lot of space."

There was no hard and fast rule about what would work at the store. Randy often worked with local craftspeople and artists, selling items on consignment when possible. They store even tried selling sex toys after people asked for them, Randy said. Joseph remembered the store tried to be discreet, selling the items in generic packages, but that didn't stop the store from being raided due to zoning codes and complaints from an adult store whose business Slacker had begun to move in on—a portent, perhaps, of things that were soon to come.

Some quick thinking by Joseph saved the day. "I pointed out the toy was simply a banana that shook. 'What's wrong with that?'" he recalled asking the inspectors innocently.

Of course, not all of the items sold were Randy's idea.

Joseph also worked with a few local graffiti artists, selling their legitimate work out of the store. One artist, he said, was able to secure a two-book deal featuring his work.

The former manager said that the store was popular with a lot of national and international musicians and bands on tour. "One day, I was working, and someone came in. I noticed his hands had all kinds of silver on them. I knew he was someone. I asked, 'Who are you?' 'Richie Havens,' he said. He was playing down the street."

Slacker's current location. *Photograph by David Rullo.*

Occasionally, bands would show up for the wrong reason. Queensrÿche, for instance, entered the store before a gig, thinking they were walking into Pittsburgh Guitars. While they were unable to find any six strings, they were taken by some of the wares available before they left.

ACTORS WHO WERE IN town filming movies would also stop by the store, he said, noting that John Malkovich was one name that stuck in his head.

Other, less desirous names also frequented the store.

Richard Baumhammers, an antisemitic white supremacist who went on a murderous rampage through several Pittsburgh communities in 2000 used to rent videos at the store. "He was one of our renters. It was brought up in his case, because his roommates said, 'He would come home and make us watch these creepy Nazi movies.' He was a major renter of these fetish Nazi movies that were legal, but there were like female Nazis beating people," Joseph said. Eventually, Baumhammers was barred from the store after he made other customers uncomfortable with his behavior.

It was another incident, however, that would cause Randy to be arrested and eventually sell the business and move to California for a period: Operation Pipe Dream.

DEE'S CAFÉ SITS ACROSS the street from both Slacker and the Beehive. It was a community bar long before it began receiving awards as the city's top dive bar, a title it embraces.

Dee's began as the type of bar that was familiar in Pittsburgh, meaning it was open early and late for the different shifts of workers at the various mills, had cheap alcohol and even featured a full menu and salad bar. It eventually evolved as needs dictated, adding pool tables and music in an attempt to cater to and reach the Gen X crowd that was beginning to call the South Side home. Or, as Andrew Laswell put it, "Dee's transitioned from an old man's bar to an old man and freak's bar. The original old men have hung on. Some of them are still there. Now, there are new old men, but the originals aren't tattooed and mutilated like the rest of us."

The bar was soon thought of as the "adult" version of the Beehive, where patrons could purchase alcoholic drinks in an environment similar to the one at the coffeehouse.

Valerie Gatchell-Christofel said that a special relationship developed between the employees at the bar and the cafe. "For several years, we would sort of collaborate with Dee's. If you had no place to go for Thanksgiving or Christmas, you could come to Dee's with a covered dish," she remembered. "Everyone could be together."

Brian Rose said that for a long time, Dee's was "the only acceptable bar" for the Beehive crowd.

Dee's was another space where one could find artists who didn't necessarily hang out at the Beehive, according to Damon Griffith. "For me, it was a conduit. It was a good place to meet other people and engage in other projects and experiences and to find out where the party's at," he said.

His wife, Sabrina, said it was the other place they could claim as their own. "For myself, coming out of art school and literally not having two dimes to rub together while trying to raise a family on the South Side, it was another place with interesting stuff and people who were in the spot I was in. You could go in there and get multiple cheap beers," she said.

UP AND DOWN EAST Carson Street, businesses were soon opening or finding renewed life, thanks to the influx of new faces there that was partially due to the Beehive and the scene that developed around it. Nick's Fat City and the Rex Theater both featured local bands, as did numerous other local bars. Street vendors served Chinese food in parking lots long before food trucks were part of the Pittsburgh landscape. Art galleries and supply stores, restaurants, theaters and even other coffeehouses all found a home in the neighborhood.

For many, the golden age of the South Side ended when the South Side Works was built on the former J&L Steel. Opened in 2002, the large shopping center featured a movie theater and stores aimed at an upscale clientele that included neither the young artists and their friends who had been visiting the neighborhood since the early '90s nor the families that had previously lived and worked in the community.

"There had always been this idea that maybe the mills would come back or that industry might return to the South Side," David Gruen said. "When I walked there, right as they were finishing up the South Side Works, it was a Charlton Heston *Planet of the Apes* moment—'You bastards. You did it. You blew it all up,'" he said.

And while he's happy for the region, noting that before the Beehive, the South Side still included a lot of closed and boarded-up businesses, the success of the coffeehouse and the scene built around it might have had an unintended consequence. "Now, it's a victim of its own success," he said.

David noted that if you drive down East Carson Street on any given weeknight now, you are more likely to be confronted by litter and groups of interlopers interested in only the availability of bars and alcohol—unlike the previous generation who sought to build something on the South Side.

OAKLAND WAS ALSO EXPERIENCING changes. The Electric Banana, a Pittsburgh mainstay that featured both local and national acts in a decaying building, closed, leaving a CBGB-sized hole in the music scene. Graffiti, another concert venue whose lineup, at one time or another, included everything from progressive rock act Fates Warning to hardcore metal act Life of Agony and a pre-hit Goo Goo Dolls, as well as local bands like Rusted Root and Kelly Affair, closed, becoming a private garage to the son of Dick Mellon Scaife, the conservative newspaper publisher.

As more and more hospitals were bought as part of the nonprofit behemoth UPMC and the area universities, Carlow College, Carnegie Mellon University, Chatham University and the University of Pittsburgh, the façade of both Forbes and Fifth Avenues, the main thoroughfares in the neighborhood, were slowly altered.

The Upstage, a goth dance club that was popular among both undergraduates and the art crowd around the city, closed, as did local eateries and independent businesses, like Jay's Book Stall, a one-time employer of writer Michael Chabon. Left in their place were trendy chains—smash burgers, quick Asian restaurants and university bookstores—that catered to the new community.

For most, the altered face of the neighborhoods they haunted during their youth signified an end of an innocent and pure era that can never be replaced.

For Randy Przekop, the '90s ended more knavishly. They ended on September 11, 2001.

12

A BAD TRIP

OPERATION PIPE DREAMS

The end of the '90s was 9/11," according to Randy Przekop. Przekop is the founder and former owner of Slacker, an alternative fashion store that was a neighbor to the Beehive coffeehouse for most of the 1990s. "Operation Pipe Dream stemmed from that," he said. "That's when Attorney General John Ashcroft felt that he could get away with things."

In fact, following 9/11, the deadliest terrorist attack on American soil, President George Bush signed into law the Patriot Act, which expanded the power of the federal government and the Justice Department to investigate crimes. Most of the expansions were related to terrorism, but the powers of the bill were broad and were, no doubt, used to investigate other criminal activities, especially those related to drugs.

It's important to remember that in the early 2000s, there was still a war on drugs that had been declared by President Ronald Reagan and his wife, Nancy. The slogan was "Just say no," but since the declaration, the federal government had no problem twisting the arms of those who didn't comply voluntarily, forcing them to fall into line.

It wasn't until 2016 that then–Pennsylvania governor Tom Wolf signed several bills legalizing the use of medical marijuana in the state. Until then, those who sold any paraphernalia that could be used to smoke marijuana were considered criminals.

Randy was one of those criminals, as was Tommy Chong.

In 2003, Tommy Chong was an actor and comedian best known as for his partnership with Cheech Marin. The team are internationally known for their string of hit records and movies, including *Up in Smoke*, *Nice Dreams* and

Cheech and Chong's Animated Movie. Much of the pair's humor was based on the marijuana culture of the late '60s and early '70s.

By the early 2000s, Chong was no longer working with Cheech and had decided to lean into his on-brand popularity by funding Chong Glass/Nice Dreams, a company started by his son that distributed bongs, water pipes and other paraphernalia, including small pipes that were sold by Randy at Slacker and other stores in the Pittsburgh region.

On the morning of February 24, 2003, Randy was awoken by nearly a dozen local, state and federal agents who had come to arrest him as part of Operation Pipe Dreams, a nationwide investigation that targeted businesses selling drug paraphernalia. He was one of the fifty-five people indicted in the operation. Slacker, Tela Ropa and other "head stores" throughout the area were almost an afterthought for the federal government, which targeted Chong because of his celebrity status.

In the end, Randy and all the other local store owners avoided prison time. Instead, he received a twelve-month sentence: six months of house arrest and six months of probation. Tela Ropa owner Kevin Jauseen was similarly sentenced: two years of probation, including three months of home detention. Slacker employee Joseph Rembiz was also detained by federal agents but walked away without charges. "They had me listed as the seller," he said, "but they let me go because it was Randy they wanted."

As for Chong, after a fine of $12 million, he received a plea deal in exchange for the non-prosecution of his wife and son. The comedian was sentenced to nine months in federal prison, a fine of $20,000, the forfeiture of $103,514 and the loss of all merchandise seized during the raid of the business.

For Randy, mounting legal bills and dwindling sales brought on by the drug bust, as well as employees who didn't want to change their lifestyles because of the charges, meant he had a difficult decision. He sold the store in 2017 to former employees and moved to California for a time.

Ironically, he pointed out, despite Pennsylvania legalizing medical marijuana, no federal laws have changed since his arrest two decades ago. Maybe because of that, he said, his biggest regret is that he did not go directly back into the business. "Because everywhere else, it wasn't a problem," he noted. "For everyone else, there was no problem. I just couldn't do it. Now, Slacker sells pipes."

And as for whether or not he's bitter at his change of fortune over the years, Randy is direct. "Given the fact that every store that has been in my former location is a pipe store, I would have to say yes. I roll over in my grave every time another pipe store opens there."

13

THE END OF AN ERA

The Oakland Beehive closed in 2001. Co-owner Scott Kramer said the location struggled during its near decade of operation, running a deficit that was made up through the profits of the South Side location. In its final year in operation, it was finally able to get out of the red, clearing $60,000, hardly a windfall.

Scott said that over the years, they had been able to talk the owners of the building into cutting their rent as they worked to create a profitable business. Their final year, a new lease had to be negotiated, and the two teams—the landlord on one side and Scott and Steve on the other—attempted to figure out a fair monthly lease. Scott thought they were near a deal several times. In the end, they couldn't come to an agreement, and Scott and Steve closed the Beehive.

The pair devoted their time to the South Side location; the Lava Lounge, which, over time, came to be known as the Tiki Lounge; and, eventually, the Double Wide Grill, a restaurant and bar that had locations on the South Side in North Huntingdon and Cranberry, suburbs of the city (all but the East Carson Street location would close during the COVID-19 lockdowns).

The South Side Beehive expanded and contracted over the years. It grew to include as many as three different rooms and then shrank to its initial footprint. Scott and Steve spent a few years operating the coffeehouse as an internet café. They added alcohol to the menu, as well, something many saw as the final act for the café. "It never really worked," Steve said, "because

BEEHIVE COFFEE FAREWELL WEEK

IT'S THE END OF AN ERA. LETS CELEBRATE.

MONDAY NOV. 19TH

GUEST COFFEE SLINGERS
12:00 TO 2:00 PM ARVIN CLAY • 6:30 TO 9:00 PM KEVN BROWN • 7:30 TO 10:00 PM MONICA McANDREW

7:30 PM MAGIC THE GATHERING MEETS BEEHIVE
Meet your friends and have one last game.
Fresh baked cookies provided to players courtesy of the Double Wide Grill

TUESDAY NOV. 20TH

GUEST COFFEE SLINGERS
6:30 TO 9:00 PM JEFF MURRAY • 7:30 TO 10:00 PM ANDREW LASWELL

7:00 PM BEEHIVE PINBALL TOURNAMENT
We are bringing back some of the old machines once housed at the
Oakland or Southside Beehive. Beehive league players, it's a reunion.
Sign ups start at 7:00 pm just before the tournament starts at 7:30

WEDNESDAY NOV. 21ST

GUEST COFFEE SLINGERS • 12:00 TO 2:00 PM ARVIN CLAY • 7:30 TO 10:00 PM NATALIE GILCHRIST

7:30 PM CHESS CLUB WITH KUMAR
B.Y.O.Board if you have one.
Players of all skills and levels are welcome.

THURSDAY NOV. 22ND

CLOSED FOR THANKSGIVING

FRIDAY NOV. 23RD

7:00 TO 10:00 PM
GOTHS AND PUNKS REUNION NIGHT
BLACK COFFEE AND ANGST
A DJ collaboration in the spirit of the Oakland
days. When the goths, punks, and everybody
in between came together, upstairs.
WITH DJS ARVIN CLAY AND KELLY DAY

10:00 PM TO ?
90S (ALTERNATIVE) DANCE PARTY
BRING YOUR REQUESTS AND YOUR CLOVES.

COFFEE AND CIGARETTES
Rekindle your old habits from 12 AM - 2AM

THE MAIN EVENT SATURDAY NOV. 24TH

GUEST COFFEE SLINGERS
11:00 TO 2:00 PM GREG REYING • 2:00 TO 5:00 PM KEITH STOCKWELL

12:00 - 4:00 PM BEEHIVE STORY TIME AND SPOKEN WORD OPEN MIC • HOSTED BY SPAZ
Join Spaz for story time, discussion, spoken word and improvisation, poetry, share old zines
sketchbooks and artwork from a time so dear in our hearts. Cheerleaders are welcome. *We
will be video documenting this segment for historical preservation for all eternity.

5:00 - 9:30 PM ART PERFORMANCES, CIRCUS ACTS, CURIOSITIES, LIVE BANDS,
ACOUSTIC ACTS, THROWBACK BEEHIVE FOOD AND DRINK MENU AND MUCH MORE.
5:00 BINGO QUIXOTE. 5:30 THE HAMER SISTERS. 6:00 GEORGE ANDREWS AND BUCKY GOUDA.
6:30 SLIPPY THE CLOWN AKA DAVID APOCALYPSE. 7:00 BREAK FOR COFFEE.
7:30 CHELSEA JONES. 8:00 CATFISH ROW. 8:30 PHAT MAN DEE. 9:00 MICROWAVES
10:00 - ? 90S RAVE AND BEEHIVE AFTER HOURS PARTY. ONE LAST TIME WITH DJ KELLY CARTER

12:00 AM - 2:00 AM COFFEE AND CIGARETTES Rekindle your old habits

SUNDAY NOV. 25TH

GUEST COFFEE SLINGERS
11:00 TO 2:00 PM VALLERY TEST AND NICHOLE • 2:00 TO 5:00 PM METAL MARY

5:00 TO 8:00 PM FilmTrip
REMEMBERING 8 YEARS OF SCREENING FILMS
Spend time flipping through old beehive film
schedules, fliers, reviews and other mementos.

8:00 TO ? AM
80S NIGHT WITH DJ EZ LOU

* scheduled performers, set times or events are still subject to change at any time.

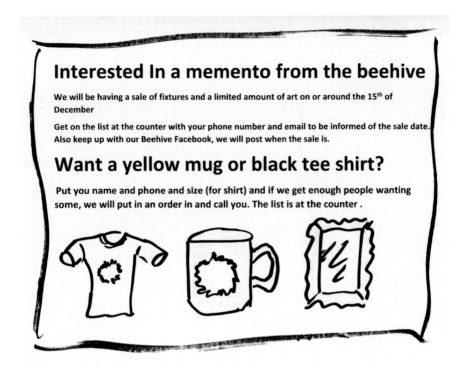

Interested In a memento from the beehive

We will be having a sale of fixtures and a limited amount of art on or around the 15th of December

Get on the list at the counter with your phone number and email to be informed of the sale date. Also keep up with our Beehive Facebook, we will post when the sale is.

Want a yellow mug or black tee shirt?

Put you name and phone and size (for shirt) and if we get enough people wanting some, we will put in an order in and call you. The list is at the counter .

Opposite: Beehive Coffee's Farewell Week list of events. *Scott Kramer and Steve Zumoff, private collection.*

Above: Scott and Steve gave their loyal customers the first opportunity to acquire Beehive memorabilia. *Scott Kramer and Steve Zumoff, private collection.*

you have the customers that don't want to be at a bar or be around drunk people." Indoor smoking bans, he pointed out, didn't help.

In the end, Steve said that everything they did to create more business opportunities simply made the situation worse.

When the building that had housed the café since it opened in 1991 was sold, Scott and Steve saw the writing on the wall. Higher rent and a dwindling customer base meant that they would have to close the café.

In September 2018, the pair posted a message on their Facebook page, announcing that they were closing the seminal coffeehouse. "It's sad to deliver this news, but the Beehive will be closing in the near future," they wrote. "We have all had some great times there, met awesome people, worked on art projects, drank lots of coffee, played countless games of pinball, to mention a few activities at the Beehive. Customers and employees were able to be themselves and be around others that had similar beliefs. We have seen kids

BYE BYE BEEHIVE

BY **AMANDA WALTZ** // AWALTZ@PGHCITYPAPER.COM

AFTER 28 YEARS in operation, the Beehive Coffeehouse and Dessertery is preparing to close for good, putting an end to a Pittsburgh institution that long served as a refuge for local artists and a hip hangout spot for the city's youth. But it's not leaving without a bang.

From Mon., Nov. 19 through Sun., Nov. 25, Beehive hosts a week of favorite activities, including chess and pinball tournaments, a weekend of retro dance nights and live performances, and, of course, coffee.

"These are all things we've done over the years squeezed into a week," Scott Kramer, Beehive co-owner, says.

Kramer and Steve Zumoff opened the Beehive in 1991 as one of the first coffeehouses in Pittsburgh. The business helped bring coffeehouse culture to the city years before it became the norm.

"[Customers] didn't know what a cappuccino was," Kramer recalls about their early days.

He says the business grew into a sort of community center for creative South Side denizens, many of them graduates of the Art Institute, who, at the time, seemed out of place in the then blue-collar family neighborhood.

Kramer expects to see a lot of old faces at Beehive's last big hurrah, including former employees who were invited to serve as guest "coffee slingers" for one last shift. "We hired a lot of really creative people," says Kramer. "It really connected a lot of artsy people who went on to do more."

One of those people is Pittsburgh avant-garde jazz singer Phat Man Dee (real name Mandy Kivowitz-Delfaver). She started hanging out at the Beehive in 1992 during her high school days, then went on to work as a janitor at the South Side Beehive and its Oakland location before it shut down in 2002.

CONTINUES ON PG. 8

Above: "Bye Bye Beehive," *Pittsburgh City Paper*, November 14, 2018. *Scott Kramer and Steve Zumoff, private collection.*

Opposite: The Beehive's sign advertising ice cream. *Scott Kramer and Steve Zumoff, private collection.*

grow up there to be adults and lost close friends and customers." They noted that, after twenty-eight years and a changing business environment, it was time to close the doors.

There were 664 replies to that message in the days immediately following the post, proving that the coffeehouse continued to maintain a large and loyal fanbase, even if they didn't still patronize the café as frequently as they did in their youth.

The actual date of the closure was a moving target. At the end of September 2018, Scott and Steve said they were targeting January 2019 but would be planning a week's worth of activity to commemorate the coffeehouse in November 2018.

By October, plans started to form, as Kelly Day posted a flyer for one last game night at the Beehive on November 19.

Kelly was born in Pittsburgh but spent most of her childhood in California with her mother. She eventually returned east and settled in Sharpsburg, a northern community along the Allegheny River. "I remember the first time I went to the South Side Beehive, sometime in '91 or '92. I must have been fourteen or fifteen years old and was like, 'Oh, my God!' I remember all the smoke. It was the middle of the day but felt like nighttime," she said.

While her first exposure to Beehive culture was at the South Side location, it was the Oakland location where she spent most of her time due to its proximity. Kelly was a DJ at WPTS, a noncommercial radio station owned by the University of Pittsburgh. She also hung out with what she called "other nonracist skinhead and ska kids" in the city's East End.

As an adult, Kelly established herself in the arts community, designing a program called Kid City Rockers, in which she DJs for kids. The program was well received. She had a residency at the Andy Warhol Museum and spun tracks for dance parties at the Children's Museum of Pittsburgh.

The mother of three now lives in Canada with her husband.

Kelly helped plan the final week of programming at the coffeehouse, but she makes it clear that she was just one part of the larger community. "I feel like there are a handful of us that aren't connected but had a piece of compiling the information and synching it all up," she said. "There was a lot that Scott had planned. He had his own vision about what bands would play, and I was like, 'Great, because I can't do that.'"

Called Beehive Coffeehouse Farewell Week: It's the End of an Era. Let's Celebrate, the activities took place from November 19 to 25. They hit all of the high notes in the coffeehouse's history and included guest coffee slingers, a night devoted to *Magic: The Gathering*, a pinball tournament, a chess tournament, a goth night and a dance party, a discussion about some of the films screened at the Oakland Beehive, performances by bands and Circus Apocalypse and a Beehive story time and open mic that included not just poetry but also people's memories of their time at the coffeehouse.

Liz Berlin, now an established solo performer and entrepreneur since her days in Rusted Root during the early years of the Beehive, performed during the week. "It was Mandy that let me know what was going on that last week," she remembered. "I ended up performing. That was hard. It was special."

Berlin's former bandmate Jenn Wertz also performed during that celebratory week. "It was sad. It was hard," she said.

While he acknowledged the finality of the day, Chuck Owsten, who played with his band Cigar Bar Riff Raff, said the night was meaningful in a different way for him. "It was something special, something I always wanted to do, play that kind of music, a Memphis jug band sound, at the Beehive. I felt like I reached my peak playing then. It was so positive," he said.

The legacy of the Beehive was also captured for posterity. The Senator John Heinz History Center, which shares the stories of Western Pennsylvania, became the curator of much of the Beehive's memorabilia. It also agreed to house an oral history of the café that was recorded by anyone who wished

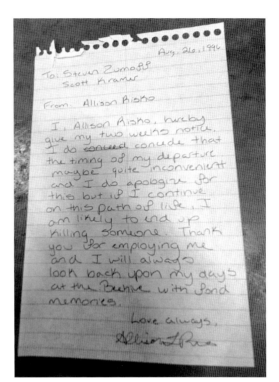

Right: A resignation letter. *Scott Kramer and Steve Zumoff, private collection.*

Below: The former home of the Beehive is once again seeking a tenant. *Photograph by David Rullo.*

to talk about the Beehive during its Farewell Week. Both Phat Man Dee and public radio station WESA's arts and culture reporter Bill O'Driscoll interviewed those who wished to be included in the audio document.

O'Driscoll served double duty during the week. In addition to recording the memories of the Beehive's patrons, he, along with several other local media outlets, including the *Pittsburgh Post-Gazette* and the *Pittsburgh City Paper*, covered the closing of the coffeehouse. The Beehive, he said, became the signature location for the South Side and the scene that was beginning to develop when it opened. "The seeds of gentrification were happening with Mario's and things like that but sort of signified what was happening," he said.

For Scott Kramer, Farewell Week was a chance to reconnect with old employees, customers and even those who had been banned, he noted with a laugh.

Everyone who attended, he said, wanted something to remember the coffeehouse by. People bought T-shirts, mugs and postcards. They also left behind something for Scott and Steve, signing a farewell book.

Especially significant for Scott was seeing the old employees back behind the counter, some after twenty-five years after they had left.

"Kelly Day did a great job putting it together and promoting it," he said.

The Beehive officially emptied its coffee pots for the last time in February 2019.

IN HIS ROLE AS an art and culture reporter and in his two decades living on the South Side on Eleventh Street, beginning in 1993, O'Driscoll gained a perspective on the neighborhood's growth that was not held by many. "I wasn't there in the '80s, but from what I understand, it was a pretty run-down place," he said. "It was hollowed out. Certainly, no one went there to party."

In the '90s, O'Driscoll said, the South Side was in a transitional phase. It was economically struggling, but it was home to underground art spaces and "the people that could afford to live there—the artists and punk rockers."

And by the end of the decade, gentrification had taken place. The house he bought for $30,000, he said, would sell for $300,000. The older generations, he noted, the ones who had worked in the steel mills and lived through their collapse, made connections to the new generation who moved in and watched as their neighbors sold their homes to flippers. The neighborhood soon became something different than what it was, like when the Beehive opened and during its golden era.

That time and place, O'Driscoll said, no longer exists and can't be recaptured. "In '91, through the late '90s, people didn't have laptops and cellphones. You walked in off the street, you got some coffee, they had food and prepackaged food and baked goods, and you hung out. You picked up some of the papers laying around and just sat there doing your own thing or until somebody wanted to talk to or someone you knew came in," he said.

Randy Przekop, too, believes that the neighborhood shifted when there were more renters than families who had lived in the community for decades. "It all changed when it became a renters-only neighborhood," he said. "It used to be an old lady babushka neighborhood, and now it's mostly rentals. The maintenance is no longer done. East Carson Street hasn't seen any investment in the buildings. In fact, we get the occasional cave-in now. The façades fall off. Nobody's making enough money to invest it and clean up the street."

For Theo Logos, the Beehive's closing was like the death of his youth. "That was such a pivotal place, especially as I established myself in Pittsburgh. The Beehive was a huge part of my life, where I met family and friends and collaborators," he said. "I used to tell people that the South Side in the '90s was the equivalent of San Francisco in the '60s. Some of my best memories and craziest stories happened there. It was touchstone, and now there's a hole, like when a parent dies."

The decision to close the coffeehouse marked the end of an era but was understandable, ventured Brian Rose. "If you're Steve and Scott and you own some bars on the South Side, how do you pay attention to a coffeehouse? The margin isn't there. The Beehive wasn't reinventing itself anymore," he said. "The foundation started to crumble. It's crazy to look back all of the people that used to be there."

Rose noted that several of the original customers had started to die and said that if the owners hadn't made the decision when they did, the pandemic would have most likely forced them to close the doors. "Nothing lasts forever," he said.

Steve laments the fact that the business he and Scott built and that lasted for nearly three decades couldn't sustain itself. "I wish it could have continued. Maybe my kids could have run it, but they're still ten years away," he said. "It would have been cool if it could have remained forever, but it wasn't making money in the end."

For Scott, the magic seemed to disappear over the last few years of the Beehive. "It just seemed like the old place just wasn't as cool as it had been," he said. Many of the employees, who worked there because of the

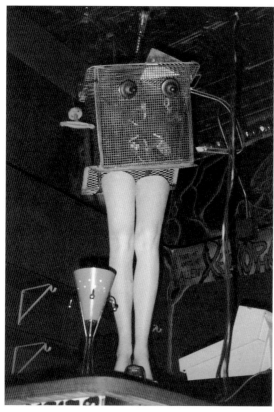

Left: "She's got legs…" Oakland Beehive artwork. *Photograph by Nikole Boyda McGinness.*

Below: Beehive Coffee's "end of an era" flyer. *Scott Kramer and Steve Zumoff, private collection.*

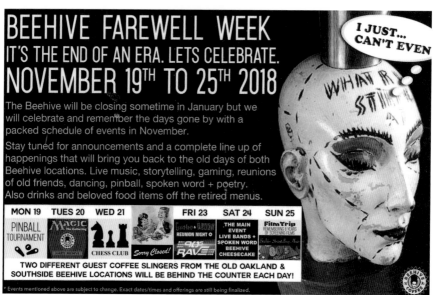

coffeehouse's reputation rather than the paycheck, were still committed to keeping the vibe going. But Scott said he grew tired as the neighborhood changed. "The community was growing up. A lot of the regulars graduated, got married and moved on," he said. "Maybe we just fell out of style."

When they decided to shut down the coffeehouse, Scott said, it was time. "I knew Steve was ready. By then, I missed all the regulars. It all seemed so quiet. All the craziness was gone," he said.

THE LEGACY OF THE BEEHIVE

Uptown Coffee. 802 Bean Company. Black Forge Coffee. Carnegie Coffee Company. Potomac Station. Delanie's Coffee. Big Dog Coffee. Yinz Coffee. Redhawk Coffee Roasters. The list goes on and on and on.

There are so many coffeehouses in Pittsburgh that every day, it seems another online publication posts a story titled "The 25 Best Coffeeshops in Pittsburgh" or "45 Pittsburgh Coffeeshops to Grab a Delicious Brew." Nearly every neighborhood in the region has at least one independently owned coffeehouse selling hot and cold espresso drinks, desserts and Italian sodas. That's in addition to the ever-present corporate behemoth Starbuck's.

Each of these coffeehouses has art created by local artists hanging on its walls or a mix of mismatched tables, chairs, cups, mugs and saucers. Some have games, like chess and checkers, sitting next to shelves filled with books. A billboard typically hangs in the corner, advertising plays, concerts and musicals. On any given night, buskers with guitars or full bands serenade those who are grabbing a cup of coffee.

The internet and social media have changed the way people interact with the coffeehouse, which is no longer the hub for meeting and making friends or planning projects. Usually, customers drift in and out, their heads down, directed at the virtual space they carry in their pockets. On a good day, however, the phones are silenced, and people talk among groups of friends. It's not the same as it was in the '90s, when cross-table talk pollinated the next art project, but coffeehouses still encourage interaction.

The Beehive's exterior. *Still taken from a video recorded by Terence Lee.*

Without a doubt, every coffeehouse in the city owes a debt to the Beehive and its visionary owners, Scott Kramer and Steve Zumoff. It was in their coffeehouse that a million ideas were born, artists met, children were raised, music was performed. It seems almost silly to say—but coffee was also consumed.

That coffee, too, was unique for the time. Steve remembered a letter the pair received shortly after opening. "It said, 'Ninety-nine cents for a cup of coffee! You won't last two weeks.' We used it as an ad in Pittsburgh back in the day," he said.

Pittsburgh itself is different from when Scott and Steve first opened the doors to the Beehive. In the early '90s, most articles written about the city talked of its postindustrial crisis. There were concerns over the brown fields the decaying steel mills were leaving behind and fears over whether the neighborhoods that, for the first time in generations, wouldn't have an economic base from the legacy of a Carnegie or Frick or some other industrial baron, could recover.

East Carson Street, formerly home to the type of storefronts that catered to a community of ex–steel workers, is now composed mostly of bars and restaurants. Its customer base is transitory and no longer defines

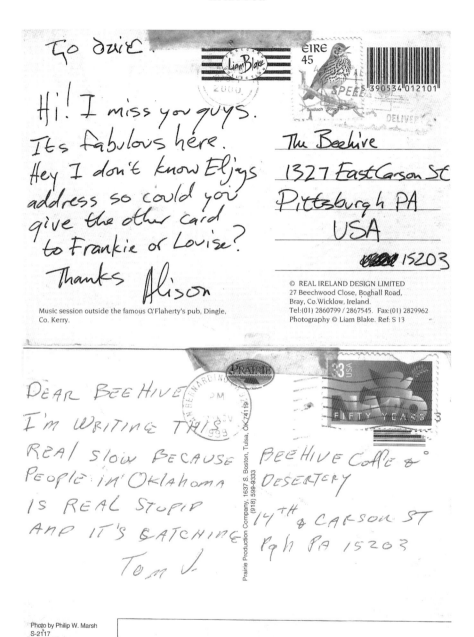

Go daire.

Hi! I miss you guys.
Its fabulous here.
Hey I don't know Eljys
address so could you
give the other card
to Frankie or Louise?
Thanks Alison

The Beehive
1327 East Carson St
Pittsburgh PA
USA
15203

Music session outside the famous O'Flaherty's pub, Dingle,
Co. Kerry.

© REAL IRELAND DESIGN LIMITED
27 Beechwood Close, Boghall Road,
Bray, Co.Wicklow, Ireland.
Tel:(01) 2860799 / 2867545. Fax:(01) 2829962
Photography © Liam Blake. Ref: S 13

DEAR BEEHIVE
I'M WRITING THIS
REAL SLOW BECAUSE
PEOPLE IN OKLAHOMA
IS REAL STUPID
AND IT'S CATCHING
Tom J.

BEEHIVE Coffe &
DESERTERY
14TH & CARSON ST
Pgh PA 15203

Prairie Production Company, 1637 S. Boston, Tulsa, OK 74119
(918) 599-9333

Photo by Philip W. Marsh
S-2117
CP20892

Postcards sent to the Beehive. *Scott Kramer and Steve Zumoff, private collection.*

171

Scott and Steve in and out of a Beehive window. *Scott Kramer and Steve Zumoff, private collection.*

the neighborhood. In fact, other neighborhoods that used the South Side as a model have come and gone and are now being replaced by newer neighborhoods where artists can afford to rent a home, start a gallery and find inspiration and materials among the decaying structures that they are slowly bringing back to life.

After decades of ridicule, Pittsburgh is now most commonly found on lists with titles like "The Best Places to Live" and "The Top Cities to Love." Some of the largest technology and healthcare institutions in the world have headquarters there, as do numerous colleges and universities. In addition, it has an art scene that rivals that of any large city throughout the world.

In many ways, the Beehive is a part of that legacy, as well.

Scott and Steve proved that you could bring new life to a community that has been written off by most of the world. Ancillary businesses created a foundation that grew out of the neighborhood, touching not just the South Side and Oakland but also all the different communities the first generation of Beehive customers migrated to: Sharpsburg, East Liberty, Lawrenceville, Hazelwood and Allentown.

Artists like Rick Bach and Michael Lotenero forged a path to success, as did musicians like Rusted Root.

BOB O'CONNOR
COUNCILMAN, CITY OF PITTSBURGH

510 City- County Building, Pittsburgh, Pennsylvania 15219 / (412) 255-8965 255- 2142

June 10, 1997

Mr. Scott Kramer
Beehive Oakland Inc.
3807 Forbes Avenue
Pittsburgh, PA 15213

Dear Scott:

Congratulations on being named one of "Pittsburgh's Top 50 Cultural Brokers" by the Pittsburgh Post-Gazette. It is indeed an honor to be listed as one of the most influential people in the city and this recognition is truly a testament to your hard work and dedication to the people of Pittsburgh. The contributions of capable individuals such as yourself is what makes Pittsburgh one of the most culturally rich cities in the nation.

You bring a great deal of excitement to the city with your innovative and fun coffee shops and now the Lava Lounge. Good luck, and thanks for doing business in the city.

I wish you continued success in future endeavors.

Sincerely,

Bob O'Connor
Councilman

BOC/bas

C:\WINDOWS\BARBARAJ\BARBIEGEN97.R.NETOPFIN.DOC

A City of Pittsburgh congratulations letter signed by then–Pittsburgh mayor Bob O'Connor, recognizing Scott and Steve as one of the city's "Top 50 Cultural Brokers." *Scott Kramer and Steve Zumoff, private collection.*

Name: Scott Kramer, 33; Steve Zumoff, 32.

Occupation: Owners of the Beehive Coffeehouse and Dessertery, South Side; the Beehive Big Screen Movie Theater, Oakland; and Lava Lounge, South Side.

Background: Kramer and Zumoff met while getting their degrees at Pitt in the late '80s. Zumoff, from Harrisburg, was managing the Oakland bar Zelda's, and Kramer, from Squirrel Hill, was making tie-dye T-shirts when the friends ventured cross-country to Hawaii to see the Jerry Garcia Band. Along the way, they gathered business ideas by stopping at every coffeehouse in sight.

Claim to fame: The South Side Beehive, which opened in February '91, let Pittsburgh know it was time to wake up and smell the coffee. It started the trend here in a funky, artistic way that still has yet to be matched. With their second shop in Oakland, the Kramer-Zumoff team also preserved the former site of the King's Court as a movie theater. By opening the Lava Lounge last October, they were the first to jump on the new wave of martini lounges. They're currently looking for their next frontier.

Scott Kramer, top, and Steve Zumoff

Left: "Pittsburgh Top 50 Cultural Power Brokers," *Pittsburgh Post-Gazette*, June 8, 1997. *Scott Kramer and Steve Zumoff, private collection.*

Below: (*From left to right*): John Zielinski, David Rullo (author), Greg Damjanovic and Rob Marsilli. This photograph was taken shortly after the Beehive announced it would be closing. *David Rullo, private collection.*

The Beehive is a part of Pittsburgh culture, even if most people don't recognize it as such.

Seen from five thousand feet above, Scott is philosophical about the legacy he and Steve left behind. "There was the early time when all of the artists were there. Later, other people came. In Oakland, there was period where the techno kids all came with wide pants. Things change. You keep trying to do things and you hope it catches on." Or as Steve said in his typical deadpan way, "There was a lot of history there."

ABOUT THE AUTHOR

David Rullo is an award-winning journalist and senior writer at the *Pittsburgh Jewish Chronicle*. His work has appeared in national and international newspapers, magazines and literary journals. He has spent the better part of five decades exploring and contributing to the city's art and literary scene. Rullo's work has been exhibited and heard in Pittsburgh's cultural district, and his bands Digital Buddha, Architects of the Atmosphere and Centrale Electrique have explored the boundaries between electronic music, spoken word, performance art and experimental music. His music can be heard in the score for the art film *The Pittsburgh Nude Project*. Rullo's collection of poetry, *Tired Scenes from a City Window*, was published in 2015. A Pittsburgh native, he lives with his wife and son in the city's South Hills, where he enjoys strong coffee, good bourbon and great books.